WORD CAIRNS

A COLLECTION OF WRITINGS

JAN VICKERY KNOST

authorHOUSE®

AuthorHouse™
1663 Liberty Drive
Bloomington, IN 47403
www.authorhouse.com
Phone: 1 (800) 839-8640

Published by AuthorHouse 12/22/2015

ISBN: 978-1-5049-6098-4 (sc)
ISBN: 978-1-5049-6099-1 (hc)
ISBN: 978-1-5049-6097-7 (e)

Library of Congress Control Number: 2015918604

CONTENTS

This book is dedicated to our children –

Keith William Knost
Kristan Beth Knost
Jana Marcy Knost
Amy Kathryn Knost

And our grandchildren –

Meghan Elizabeth Battiloro
Patrick Michael Connor III
Haley Bridget Connor
Katherine Jan McCarthy
Christopher Zachary Battiloro
Linnea Faith Battiloro
Jensen Cole Butler
Jonah Nathaniel Butler
Anna Brielle Butler

With incredible love and gratitude,
Jan and Lorna Knost

Many people, especially ignorant people,
want to punish you for speaking the truth,
for being earnest, for being you.

Never apologize for being correct or for
being years ahead of your time.

If you're right and you know it, speak your
mind. Speak your mind even if you are a
minority of one.

The truth is still the truth.

- Mohandas Gandhi

FOREWORD

- by Jana Marcy Knost Battiloro;
daughter of The Reverend Jan Vickery Knost

"He was a man. Take him for all in all. I shall
not look upon his like again."

- Hamlet, Act 1, Scene 2

Easter Sunday – the "show of shows" so to speak in a minister's church year -the Sunday when even the most apathetic church-goers find the time to dust off their Sunday best and come for some spiritual soul food. My father was never in the pew with my mother and us. Since I was born he has always been "up there" – giving a sermon, saying a prayer, giving "the show". This particular Easter Sunday I want to tell you about was no different, except this time I got away from my mother's watchful, quiet arms. As a toddler, I did not feel the need to be cleansed or sanctified– I just wanted to walk, explore, and survey the territory. So I did. I clumsily worked my chubby toddler legs up the steps to the mystical realm of spirituality known in Christian religion as the pulpit. With absolutely no knowledge of the importance of the day or of my father's role in the pageantry, I reached my arms up to him for the opportunity to be held. He obliged, as well as continued to preach. I remained perched there, for a few moments, safely in my father's arms, listening to the cadence and tenor of his voice, surveying the sea of people and community that was my world at the age of one and a half. I glanced down to my mother and siblings, waiting in the pew below, and I'm sure I recognized many of the people who were probably amused by the temerity of this toddler. When I felt I had surveyed my world enough, I stiffened in his arms, signaling to him I was ready to move on. He let me down, gently, with the knowledge I would find my mother and I would probably explore some more before I reached her again, but that I would undoubtedly be fine and learn along the way.

It was this moment that maybe best captures my experience as the daughter of this man. How do I capture his strength, his intelligence, his creativity, his *joie de vivre*, his energy, his charisma, and his magnanimous personality in a paltry foreword for a book? I don't know. I suppose that is why I begin this as the toddler, reaching up for the safety of his arms, but knowing that he would allow me to go when I was ready, trusting my own sense of adventure and spirit to find my own way. That is who he is to us, my siblings and me.

The child of a minister learns that life is different than the lives of other children very quickly. Sundays are the busy days, whereas other dads dreaded Mondays. Saturday nights were the stressful night when Dad read the sermon to Mom, whereas other families went out or relaxed on Saturday nights. Weeknight family dinners happened later than most families, after Dad returned from one of countless committee meetings. Christmas Eve was a busy night of work and we never quite knew when he might come in and join the family celebration. Our phone number was always easy to remember, in case a parishioner needed him in an emergency. There was always a chance he would be called to a hospital late at night, there was always a stranger at our Thanksgiving table, and we would occasionally be told not to go in the living room till "Daddy finished the wedding." This is the life of a "preacher's kid," – especially this preacher's kid. I just assumed my dad was different than others because of the nature of his job. And my father is different – but thankfully, as I have aged, I recognize that what sets my father apart from any other dad is everything other than his unique career.

My father was called to the ministry because of his need for and love of people in general. He loves life and he loves people. His immense sense of caring and compassion is ebullient and infectious. My father taught us this and how to love one another and make sure we are kind and generous. My father taught me about baseball, fishing, classical music, and good writing. My father taught me about good movies, a great meal, and how to use a power drill. My father taught me to write and read poetry, to speak publicly, and to sing loudly. My father taught me to be politically attentive and socially active, to stand up when others might sit down, and to be brave in the face of adversity. My father taught me to cry out loud when I feel the need, and to laugh out loud when I feel the need. My father taught me to say "I love you" and often.

Each day he would make us breakfast, and he served us a question each morning with our food: "What do you have to look forward to today?" As a parent, myself, now I understand his meaning – to find unique in the mundane, to find joy in the sorrow, to find hope in the dread. He encouraged me my whole life to take a different view or strike a different path, trusting his lessons would guide us to safety. As a teenager, I remember driving to California on a summer vacation. As we traversed the very flat, very desolate area of West Texas, we slept on and off to break up the monotony. On one particular leg of the journey, we traveled at night. He stopped the car, woke us up, and asked us to get out and stand in the middle of the road, just to look up at the stars. I looked up at the dizzying landscape of overwhelming stars in that immense sky and heard him say, "Just look at that." Once again, he was reminding us to look again, enjoy the view, look for the good, and appreciate with humbled awe the world in which we are so privileged to be alive.

My father has been providing me with the opportunity to marvel at the view for over forty years now. I suppose it began with that Easter Sunday perched up in his arms, but I know it has not ended. My hope is that each of the pieces in his book provides you with a different view of him, in the wonderful, complex mosaic that is my father. I have learned to share him with, what has amounted to thousands of people, throughout his career. I am only so happy to have the opportunity to share him once again.

Thank you, Dad, for the lift and the view. Life is grand.

AUTHOR'S PREFACE

Gentle Reader,

Please know how happy I am that you have received this volume. I have wanted to produce it for some time. Mostly, it is because I wanted to leave something for our grandchildren to read after I have departed this mortal coil. One son-in-law once asked, "Have they ever been there when you were in the pulpit?" I had to say, "No." Then he followed with, "It would be great if you could put together a book of your work over the years."

Well, that idea "took" for me. I began to go through nearly a half-century of professional writings to find some modest offerings that may be of interest to my young grandchildren as they grow to maturity. And so, this is it.

My life has been dedicated to several very simple things: my wife and family, my profession, music, laughter and the proscenium arch, not to mention fishing and golf.

This book is a collection of sermons, minister's columns, stories and poems. They have been "resurrected" (not a Universalist theme, to be sure!) that I hope you will enjoy.

The stories are mostly from experiences in my life. The poems are statements about the human condition. The sermons are only a sampling of a much larger file of efforts made in behalf of the congregations I served. The rubric for writing each sermon was to spend an hour of research and preparation for every minute of its length.

I sincerely hope you who are not "family" will like this little volume. It is a small indication of my gratitude for having been able to enjoy life with you all through the years. With every good wish and with affection,

Jan Vickery Knost
Charlestown, RI
2015

Parish the Thought

"And one of the elders of the city said, Speak to us of Good and Evil.
And he answered:
Of the good in you I can speak, but not of the evil.
For what is evil but good tortured by its own hunger and thirst?
Verily when good is hungry it seeks food even in dark caves,
and when it thirsts it drinks even of dead waters."

Kahlil Gibran, *The Prophet*

All of us struggle with the excruciating dilemmas wrought in our world today. Suicidal terrorism continues to grip the human psyche. We feel helpless to find a way to reason with those willing to die in order to kill others.

We grieve for our sisters and brothers of the Roman Catholic faith, divided over the problems wrought by the criminal behavior of those in whom they had put their trust – priests and hierarchy alike.

Our national memory seems short when measured against the horrors of two World Wars, the Korean War and Viet Nam. Some are never able to forget.

Even our former enemies now rally with us as economic and cultural friends. I wept at saying "Goodbye" to Seiji Ozawa after his twenty-nine remarkable years as Music Director of the Boston Symphony Orchestra. One writer expressed it all: *"He's our guy!"*

I wept, too, when our babysitter, Helen Nomura, didn't come to our house anymore. She had been taken to a concentration camp in Oregon following the Japanese bombing of Pearl Harbor. But my brother and I participated in all the War Drives – savings bonds, scrap metal, rendered fats for making munitions, Victory Gardens. We hardly knew the meaning

1

of "good and evil" but the blackouts were really there on the West Coast where Dad attended seminary.

Now the new symbol of human courage and sacrifice is a picture of three firemen in NYC raising a tattered flag at Ground Zero. It has virtually replaced the seven Marines raising a flag on Iwo Jima.

The more things change, the more they remain the same.

We, who have given our lives to the work of assisting people through their religious journeys, feel just as helpless as many of you. We wish we could assure a peaceful existence and a world of good and plenty. But the evil of thirst and hunger won't go away. Not now. Not ever.

We can only open our hearts to each other's pain and dedicate each day to addressing the ills nearby, praying that sanity will come.

A PULPIT PERSPECTIVE

One morning last week, I mentioned to my wife that it was just about time for the smelt to start biting in Hingham Harbor, Massachusetts. I then alluded to the fact that salt water being but forty-five minutes away, there must be some smelt in New Jersey too. "Don't tell me you're going to do that again? We still have enough smelt from last year to last a month!"

I suspect many spouses might be saying the same thing this time of year. Smelt fishing is an enjoyable late fall and early winter pastime – still catching fish so close to the advent of winter. Yet, it reminds me of something else. I recall a strong and wonderful person named Hazel Kehoe. I am happy to say it was my privilege to know her.

Hazel was a tiny woman in her late sixties when I first met her. Live shrimp could only be purchased at the Bait Shack in Hingham, and that shack was her longtime bailiwick. She would always greet me cheerfully and mutter some observations about the "male crowd who leave beer cans on my dock." I learned that she and her husband were the proud parents of five sons. Mr. Kehoe had died some years before, but Hazel had kept his trust by raising all of them in the Roman Catholic faith. She remained a lifelong Baptist, attending church regularly, but her boys were "Catholic" – that's what he wanted.

Mrs. Kehoe could stand toe-to-toe with the roughest of the waterfront crowd who graced the docks on cold fall and winter evenings to catch the tiny smelt. One story I recall tells of the time one customer kept getting nature's "hurry-up calls." It was probably due to the large quantities of malt brew he was imbibing while fishing. Mrs. Kehoe kept watching him as he went back and forth to one of the lockers to "use-it-for-that-which-it-was-not-intended." As he stood in the door of the locker for the third time, he suddenly felt himself propelled inside by a strong shove on the back. Standing outside was this tiny woman yelling "I'll teach YOU to use these lockers for that!" as she pounded two ten-penny nails into the door to keep him there.

Religious understanding is a fragile enterprise, especially when it involves understanding someone else's religion. Too many of us let tradition get in the way of the right of others to choose. Hazel Kehoe might very well have raised her sons Baptists. But she didn't. She chose, rather, to follow the wishes of her husband. In doing so, and in quietly observing the tenets of her own faith, she showed by example that it is possible to be open to other religious faiths and the values they teach. There is not one of her sons who would deny this.

Years ago, I was honored by being asked to sit with the members of her family at the funeral service in her memory. I realized what a joy it was to have known her. She taught me something that, in reality, I often take so much for granted. It concerns the priceless possession of religious freedom that this country holds high. Would that all of us could do likewise.

Cheers, Mrs. Kehoe!
It's smelting time, again!

Some Thoughts on Suffering

Katherine Mansfield was a British writer of incredible sensitivity. She died in 1922 after suffering terribly from tuberculosis. Records of her life indicate, however, that she rose above it and became an example of courage and inspiration for countless others. In her *Journal*, she left us these words:

"I do not want to die without leaving a record of my belief that suffering can be overcome. For I do believe it. What must one do?

Do not resist. Take it. Accept it fully. Make it a part of life.

Everything in life that we really accept undergoes a change."

These are difficult words to understand or accept. Obviously, conveyed to one who may be ailing, they are apt to evoke cynicism and even bitterness. A person who is healthy may accept it but realize very little of the depth of meaning Ms. Mansfield's words have conveyed. Suffice it to say, then, that one must experience pain to be in a position to intuit the impact of her words.

Think of people you have known who have suffered. Think of figures of history in a similar vein. Beethoven must have felt that life had dealt him a brutal trick in making him deaf. (It is alleged that he finally sawed the legs off his piano so he could put his ear to the floor to feel the vibrations of its strings.)

"Do not resist. Take it. Accept it fully."

Grief often denotes a wish to escape the reality of death. The same can be said of suffering. Perhaps we can avoid it by fighting it. And yet, according to Ms. Mansfield, in accepting suffering, unexplained tragedy gives way to the larger beauty which is life. It submerges us into a sea of hope written about by poets and writers of history. It is shown in the work of artists and sculptors. It is lauded by the musician and the dancer.

Life of joy – life of pain – unexplained, often unfair and unjust, even unthinkable at times, is forever shaping us in a truer form. When we rise above the pettiness and selfishness that try to close us in, we become one with the Life Force that makes all things eternally new.

>Look life in the eye
>to see if there is something more
>compelling than the painful message
>thus conveyed;
>as yet we may see and hear no answer
>to our query as to how the strength
>to thus accept
>can come
>and yet
>somehow, and most marvelously.
>it often does…

AN ALTAR'D STATE

There were just two of us. We had planned a "shoestring" trout fishing trip to the Trinity Alps in northern California. For two days we had camped in a state facility along the stream that runs out of what is called "Hobo Gulch." On the third day, we drove up over the mountain, parked our car on a siding and began the "walk-slide-walk" down into the deepest most primitive part of the gulch, a distance I remember as being about a mile on a steep descent.

We traveled light; fishing rods, a couple of sandwiches, two beers for lunch. When we finally arrived, we discovered an awesome continuance of huge boulders all shaped in sharp angles and lines as igneous rocks can be. Some stood ten to twelve feet in height. On occasion, we'd have to clamber to the top of one to drop our lines down to a pool below where we imagined a lifetime catch might be waiting. The native rainbow trout we had been told were there cooperated beautifully. Our day was filled with "catch-and-release" tie-ups many times over. We kept two for dinner.

After lunch, the climb ahead of us being onerous in the extreme, we began our ascent back to the car. Here, let me pause to share a seldom-used word and its definition. This is crucial to the rest of the adventure. Webster defines "scree" (skre) as "a steep mass of detritus on the side of a mountain." "Detritus" is gravel produced by erosion. When one climbs up such an incline, the tendency is to gain only about a foot of progress for every two feet taken. The gravel slides out from under your feet as they propel the body upward. Very quickly, we were wet with perspiration and puffing like marathoners.

At my suggestion, we stopped to rest. Then we engaged in a more regular, less harried climb, being careful to conserve our energy in that high range of mountains. We labored for more than an hour. The mountain appeared before us on both sides, up and down as the same. There were no recognizable landmarks to indicate the mountain road was near. The distance "up" seemed the same as the distance "down."

We traversed a beautiful redwood forest for what seemed hundreds of yards. It was not an area I remembered being in before. Meanwhile, my companion continued climbing, stubbornly insisting that we were "almost there." Which we weren't! When I reached him some fifteen minutes later (He was in much better shape.), I was all but exhausted. So I sat to rest again. But he vowed to continue before I had recovered. "Don't go so fast. All we have to do is continue up. The road will be there. Slow down!"

Later, my friend admitted that he had felt a tinge of panic with the darkness coming. Then something happened. As he stood waiting for me to reach him again, he suddenly began to swat and wave his arms crazily. At first, I thought him daft. "What's the matter?" I called. "Hornets!" he cried, swatting them away again and again. When he had moved a few yards away, we assessed the damage. Four bites, not a little pain, but he was okay. No shock seemed apparent from the stings.

When we finally reached the road it was almost dark. But our walk to the car on level ground was almost leisurely. We had had a wonderful day, notwithstanding our escapades. And you know; it seems as vivid today as the day I experienced it with my lifelong friend.

I also would observe that part of the road I've traveled medically of late has been a little like that climb. "Two feet up and one back" has sort of typified my days and weeks of recovery. That's when it has been of major benefit to me to insist on keeping a positive outlook and to take the time to meditate on the gifts of experience and insight life has to give.

As Yoda might have said, "Grateful, then, I be!"

SOMETIMES A TEAR GLISTENS

Once in a while and usually, quite unexpectedly, I get the urge to cry. It is hard to explain to another. There I am, suddenly with tears in my eyes, the emotion welling up from deep within.

Music beautifully played can do it. So can the reading of some familiar poem. Occasionally, it can be the sheer joy of parenthood. Certain movies can do it. Show me scenes from *To Kill a Mockingbird, Mr. Roberts* or, more recently, *Ordinary People* or *On Golden Pond* and I dissolve.

This, then, is a call to listen a little more carefully to what our feelings are telling us. Society so often places expectations upon us that call for "right conduct." Acceding to such customs make it impossible for true emotions to get to the surface. Tears shown by men have long been thought of as a "no-no." The machismo image prevails.

How sad.

My experience in giving way to tears in a healthy display of emotion, whether from sadness, inspiration or joy, have strengthened and uplifted me, giving me a fuller knowledge of who I am.

Sometimes I will seek out a late night movie or some piece of classical music. Then, alone, safe and unseen or unheard, I can weep away. Unfortunately, this is a mite dishonest.

So the next time someone tells you that it is unhealthy or unattractive or unseemly for a grown person to show tears, I suggest you think twice about such an adage. Perhaps if more people were willing to be more honest about their emotions, society might become just a bit healthier.

Someone once said that "laughter is the sunshine of the soul." And it's true. But there's that other side, too. The side that says the inclusion of real, healthy, life-giving tears is a strong ingredient in the living of our days. They show our human side, too.

MY FIRST REAL FUNERAL

My parents didn't get a lot of time off. They were hard working professionals who denied themselves time to "rest and refresh themselves" more often than not.

While we were living in Peoria, Illinois and Dad was minister of the Universalist Church in that city, they had a chance to enjoy some time away. A wealthy couple invited them to join them at their summer home on a lake in Wisconsin and they accepted.

In getting ready to go, my dad took me aside and said, "I will be gone for two Sundays and I want you to lead the services on those Sundays. Also, if there are any deaths in the congregation, I have left you a funeral service to use. My friend, the funeral director, is a member of the church and he will guide you through the process. Just show up and follow his lead." I was sixteen years old.

Days followed. My parents were in Wisconsin enjoying their time away. Then the phone rang in our home. I answered. It was the funeral director informing me of the death of a congregant and that the family would like to have her service during the coming weekend.

Stunned and incredibly afraid, I called the number my parents had given me for Wisconsin. My mom answered.

"Mom, could I please speak to Dad?"

"Of course, son."

After a slight pause my Dad was on the line. "Yes, Jan, what's the matter?"

"Well, Dad, the director called to let me know that so-and-so died and that the service would be this Saturday at eleven o'clock."

Calmly and with a measured reply, my Dad said, "Yes, okay. I know things will go well. I gave you the service you need to read and the director will tell you just what to do when you get to the funeral home. I know it will all go well. Anything else?"

Long pause.

"Yes, Dad… but… but… but… this woman is REALLY DEAD!"

(Postscript: the service went off without a hitch notwithstanding me.)

WADIN' THE CREEK SATURDAYS

It was the summer of my thirteenth year. We were living in a tiny southern Alabama town called Brewton. It sits on the confluence of the Escambia River and Burnt Corn Creek. One day in June my new friend Almon came up to me in the school hallway.

"Wanna go with me tomorrow? I'm gonna wade the creek and do some slash fishin'."

Fishing was not a sport I had learned from my Dad. He was a preacher and had little time to take us out on the water. But this opportunity was great because Almon was a native of the area and I knew I'd learn something about "fishin'."

He came by early Saturday morning and handed me his brother's U.S. Army cartridge belt. He was wearing his. "Here, put your sandwich in these pouches and your chocolate bar and other stuff." He'd told me what I should bring the day before. Then he handed me a cane pole about seven feet long with a black piece of mill end braided line attached. At the end he had tied a small black fly I later learned was a black gnat.

We walked down the street past my Daddy's church, turned right and headed to the edge of town. The local swimming hole on the creek was named "O'Bannion's Wash Hole." (I never found out who "O'Bannion" was but it was a great place to go on hot summer days.) We waded into waist-high water and started tossing our baits to the shore, then jerking them across the top of the water. I followed Almon, waiting until he was about fifty feet ahead.

In no time he had a fish on. It was a bluegill sunfish that fought like crazy. Almon took a stick he had stuck through his belt. He threaded it through the gill of the fish and moved it down to the crotch of the "Y-shaped" fish keeper. Almon looked at me for a minute then said, cryptically, "It all depends on how you hold your mouth." I looked at him quizzically. "Do shorter jerks, boy." He turned and continued up the creek.

Finally I had a bite. And not just a bite. My rod tip bent nearly double and disappeared into the creek waters. "Wow!" I said. "I've got a whale!" When I finally subdued the fish, (not without a lot of help from my friend) I found I'd caught my first largemouth black bass.

"Great," said Almon. "That'll go over two pounds." He threaded it on my fish keeper and returned to fishing.

We continued to catch fish all morning and finally sat on the creek bank to eat our sandwiches. Then we turned for home. We each had four or five fish on our "stringers" when we got back to proudly show our Moms. That first supper of fried fish was one I will never forget. Or, indeed, those leisurely Saturdays on Burnt Corn Creek.

Then there was the time we were resting on a little sand beach when we heard some people kind of huffing and puffing. There was some quiet talk, too. We crawled through the woods to see what...

Oh, yeah, but that's another story...

HELEN

She was a beautiful, tiny lady. Jet black hair, deep brown eyes, a voice that could charm the bark off a tree and a gentle manner. Her name was Helen and she was our babysitter.

Each week she'd arrive at our home in Altadena to be with us while our parents did extra jobs since it was the depths of the Depression. Our excitement was palpable. Why? Helen liked to play. She loved to mystify us with her skills at origami, making paper storks, airplanes, animals of different kinds. All this with a simple piece of paper.

There were other ways in which she entranced us as little boys. One was for us to witness her at rehearsal. Our dad was director of an Opera Guild and Helen, being a Nisei (native Japanese-American) played the title role of *Madame Butterfly*. Her voice changed from a soft murmur as she folded each piece of paper to a beautiful soprano that made one's heart beat faster. Gosh! What a wonderful person who graced our lives in those early days.

Then December 7, 1941 arrived. I can still recall the shock on our parents' faces as they listened to the reports from Honolulu and the attack on Pearl Harbor. In no uncertain terms, our nation was declared to be "at war." The lights went out during blackouts and fear reigned.

Suddenly, too, we were without our beloved sitter. Helen was no more. She didn't come to our home to see us. She was gone. I can never forget our puzzlement at her absence. After all, we were just little boys and no explanation was forthcoming from our parents for her absence.

Later, we learned that Helen had been taken with her family to an American concentration camp for Japanese-Americans. Our government took their possessions and left them with what they could carry there, somewhere in Oregon or Washington State. She didn't get released until the war was over. And we never saw her again.

Fortunately, decades later, our mother called us both with word that she'd reached Helen. She was married, had a family, lived in San Bernardino, California and ran a travel agency with her husband. My first Christmas card to her was an inadequate missive, to be sure, considering the pain of missing her for so long. She lives in a nursing home now and her husband said she's "in a bad way." But we will always remember her otherwise – gentility, talent, beauty. Ah!

EASTER DINNER - 1942

When my brother, Peter, and I were growing up in Altadena, California, World War II was in full swing. Nevertheless, there were still a few amenities for small children to enjoy. One was a carnival that came to our little suburb. Our Dad took us. We enjoyed the various rides and lost a lot of the games. But one was a hoot. We both won a live, yellow duckling. Soon they were ensconced in our home backyard with a fenced in place to enjoy. We played with them every day, feeding them and watching as they waddled around the yard.

As the weeks went by, our two new pets grew and grew. We named them "Ducky Daddles" and "Ducky Waddles." It was a real "puppy-love-affair" for us both. Then reality bit.

Folks were asked to do the patriotic "right thing" and invite one or more servicemen to Easter dinner. My parents were true to the call. Two young sailors, waiting for their ship to leave for the war in the Pacific, arrived at our home on Easter Sunday.

What you are about to read, dear reader, is what one might describe as a child tragedy. (See the Thanksgiving scene in the movie *Giant*.) Our two ducks had reached a measurable five to six pounds apiece. My parents were not wealthy. In fact, they were quite poor. Without a second thought, and with the agreement of our mother, Dad took our two pets down to the butcher who prepared them for cooking.

When the table was set and Dad had welcomed our guests and pronounced the grace before our meal, Mom brought in a huge tray which was covered. When Dad raised the lid, there were two cooked creatures.

"Mom... what are those?" I asked.

Without so much as a nod or hesitation, and most certainly with not a scintilla of knowledge about child psychology, she said, "Why, son, those are Ducky Daddles and Ducky Waddles. We had them prepared for our young servicemen."

Obviously, I have never forgotten that moment or the sobs my brother and I brought to the table. Self-evidently, the non-adults only ate the vegetables on that momentous day.

Growing up is a bitch.

A Singing Saint's Remembrance

(J.V. Knost '56)

On Friday, January 22, 1954, the Singing Saints, a men's *a cappella* singing group of twelve singers and their director, embarked on a five-day tour to the New York City area. They had only been a group for two years emerging from a previous quartet. The founder/director, Ernest "Bill" Moncrieff, ('54) and the director of the Saint Lawrence University Alumni Office planned the itinerary. What follows is one member's recollections of those memorable days with humble apologies for lapses of personal memory in the record of what transpired.

We traveled to the Watertown, New York airport and boarded a Mohawk Airlines flight to Newark, New Jersey airport which, in those days, boasted but a single-story terminal. The Budweiser Eagle neon sign was visible to the west as we landed. It continues to be a familiar landmark of the huge Newark/New York International Airport today.

About three hours later we were "singing for our supper" at a dinner meeting of the Saint Lawrence University Alumni of the New York area. That night we were "billeted" in the homes of those same loyal "Larries" in the Westchester County area.

The next day found us singing at the Dobbs Ferry School for Girls in Dobbs Ferry, New York. Following that, we entertained the student body at Sarah Lawrence College. When we were ushered into the hall we found that one of the parents attending for the Parents' Weekend at school was none other than the famous composer/band director, Duke Ellington. His daughter was a student at Sarah Lawrence.

Our director informed us of this fact and then said, "Gentlemen, the last song we sing will be dedicated to Mister Ellington. After all, he wrote it!" We then sang *Mood Indigo* and, to be honest with you, it was one of the truly highpoints of our trip. To see the "Duke" smiling and nodding his head as we sang filled our hearts with pride.

The first night after arriving, we were guests on the *Steve Allen Show*, the first of the late night shows that was the precursor to Jack Paar, Johnny Carson, Jay Leno and David Letterman.

Appearing "in uniform" as we were, the ushers directed us to sit in the first two rows. As we were being seated we noticed that a young man was rehearsing for the show. We came to find out it was the singer Steve Lawrence. That night proved to be his debut before he and Eydie Gorme became a famous singing duo.

Once the show got started, Steve Allen asked his producer the identity of the young men in the first two rows. The producer asked that our leader stand and identify us. "Bill" Moncrieff stood and proudly announced that we were "the Singing Saints from Saint Lawrence University." There we were in our maroon blazers with Saints' logos, striped ties, white button-down shirts, charcoal slacks and cordovan shoes – all of us nervous but surprised and happy to be recognized by the famous entertainer.

Mister Allen asked if we would be willing to honor the show with a song. And so we did. As I remember, we sang two. One was *A Tribute* ('Nestling 'neath the purple shadows of the Adirondack Hills…") and the other was… well, I just don't remember.

Following the enthusiastic applause from the audience, our Business Manager, baritone Howard Crowell, ('54) asked Mister Allen if he could bring him a gift his group prepared for him. Steve, in his usual gracious manner, replied, "Of course." With that, our fellow singer was invited up onto the stage. He presented Steve with a framed picture. It read, "To Steve Allen from the student body of Saint Lawrence University. You have been voted our favorite television personality and comedian at work today. Thank you!"

Obviously, Mister Allen was touched beyond words, so much so that he placed the framed letter on his piano and played a jazz rendition to us in gratitude. (We never did hear how "Howie" Crowell had gotten hold of a typewriter and picture frame to affect such a happy presentation!!)

Following the show, everyone was put "on their own" in the big city. Several of us opted to go to Lou Walter's famous "Latin Quarter" nightclub, located at that time just behind the old Metropolitan Opera

House. (Walters was father of the famous Barbara Walters of current fame.) We arrived and found that the "cover charge" was five dollars. It could be used to buy drinks which, in those days, were priced at the incredibly impossible amount of a dollar a drink!

We sat at a semicircular table and watched the show. The headliner was someone we had only read about. Her name was Christine Jorgenson, newly returned from a Swedish sex-change operation. She entered in a long, flowing white gown and proceeded to serenade the crowd with a medley of popular songs. She received a standing ovation.

The hour, by this time, was late. We realized we had to find our way home to Scarsdale where our alumni hosts awaited our return. Unfortunately, we misread the subway signs and in the twinkling of an eye we were going in the wrong direction. No one paid much attention until the train finally stopped – in Far Rockaway! We were about as far from our destination as one could be and still have the subway at one's disposal. To add to the confusion, the stationmaster told us that we had arrived on the last train of the early morning. The next one returning to our destination would not leave for two hours!

Being the creative group we were, we didn't despair. We simply spent the remaining time waiting – and singing together.

Simply put, those few days over fifty years ago proved to be a wonderful opportunity for us as a singing ensemble to "stretch our wings" and sing for the first time away from the Saint Lawrence campus – a practice that proved to happen more and more as the years went on. What a hoot! And we still remember it with gratitude. And we know with assurance that the Singing Saints still charm their listeners as we did then with songs, songs, songs! Yes, they were the best of days.

A Spanish Reverie

Harris-Manchester College, 1958
Oxford University

We have this painting, you see. It's quite a simple depiction, being nothing more than an ancient door and a kind of shattered wall supporting it. The artist added sand to his oils where the plaster is cracked and worn. There is no doubt about the reason we acquired this work of art. It immediately reminded both of us of a door in the ancient town of Trebbiano, Italy that opened into a beautiful, modern restored apartment. Simone de Beauvoir and her sister had acquired the first of these properties with the agreement that they would leave the outer walls in their ancient 11th century condition and that they could then modernize the interior. We were there with our two older children to spend a blissful three weeks during a sabbatical study leave. It was the kindness and generosity of a Florentine Italian artist that we were given the free rent treatment.

For me, however, there was more to the substance of that painting than that wonderful dalliance. When I asked the artist in Rockport, Massachusetts where he had found the scene he gave me the name of a tiny Spanish village in the mountains that look upon the Costa del Sol beaches.

Fifty years ago a student companion and I trekked up to that village from where we were living in the tiny town of Fuengirola, a fishing village fast by the ocean. There were six of us. We were students studying at Oxford University. We had rented a nine-room villa with a muezzin tower and rose garden. It had cost us sixty dollars, American – ten dollars apiece for five weeks! Permit me to relate our adventures.

We had come down from Oxford University for the spring break. All of us agreed that to stay at home would be too expensive and that we could live in Spain for much less. I had met my friends in one of Oxford's parks. They were playing touch football and asked if I'd like to join them. I was at the University for a year of study that would lead to my degree in Theology in the United States. Touch football was their way of letting loose after their studies and we met regularly each week.

Toward the end of Trinity term sometime in March they asked if I'd like to join them in Spain for the holiday. I thought it an agreeable possibility and agreed to join them. They were all getting to Malaga, Spain by different means but they were going to meet up at the train station there on a specific date.

My trip there was memorable in itself but I shall only allude to it in the briefest of terms. I went with the captain of the Oxford University Basketball Club (on which I played) to the city of Paris. We spent four days there before I departed by train for the Spanish border. There I purchased a third class ticket that allowed me 1500 kilometers of travel anywhere in the country. The first night was spent in Barcelona; the second in Valencia where I toured what I was told was the first stock exchange in history. (I also still remember being put in a roomette on the train with a Spanish priest. We were the only passengers in it. The other sections were jammed with people but somehow, being a visitor gave us some mysterious right to travel without such crowding.) It was amazing, too, that in every Roman Catholic cathedral I entered, the tour guide claimed that *they* had the original Holy Grail. Then, for a few pesetas, they would proudly show it to me. So it goes.

The third part of my journey was on an overnight train to the city of Seville. There were eight of us in the roomette. Three of my fellow travelers were two brothers and a sister, dancers on their way to Casablanca to perform. Using halting Spanish and "pidgin" English we soon became acquainted.

At each stop, one would leave the train to purchase bottles of wine at the little wine shops outside each of the stations. A bottle of wine cost about twelve cents. If you presented the empty bottle at the next station it cost six cents to fill it! Even as a student I could afford to be the host for all my traveling companions. Self-evidently, we soon became very friendly, singing different songs together, American and Spanish. Soon, with the help from many bottles of wine, I fell asleep.

I was shaken awake by my friends. They had apparently taken pity of my drunken state and had lifted me to the luggage area above the aisle where I could stretch out, moving the luggage to the floor. I just managed to make the connecting train from Seville down to Malaga. I shall never forget the warm goodbyes of those three attractive people.

Sure enough, when I arrived in Malaga, there were already four of my Canadian friends waiting. Two more arrived soon after. We learned that we could get to our destination only by bus and so we did. We wanted to go, as I remember, to the first village past the tourist village of Torremolinos, a popular resort stop for Europeans. That village proved to be Fuengirola.

The way we achieved our rental was a story in itself. We entered what seemed to be the only taberna in town. There was a man sitting slouched at the bar. My Canadian friend, Sholto, asked him if he spoke English. He looked at us all in a kind of puzzling, yet judgmental, way and said, rather softly, "Yeah."

We asked if he knew how we might go about renting a villa.

He said, "See that guy over there?" We looked and there was a well-dressed Spaniard holding court with some friends at a table. Our new acquaintance continued, "Well, his name is Pako. And he's the closest thing to being the Mayor, the Chamber of Commerce and the Office of Real Estate in this hick town." (Fuengirola was no bigger in 1958 than an upstate New York town with the ruins of an ancient Moorish castle down the beach. Today, ruined by German tourism, I have been told that it is replete with high-rise hotels and all that such development brings.)

Another Canadian friend, John, spoke with Pako. Pako said he had a rental that he'd gladly rent to us. It was just down the street and only a couple of blocks from the beach. We said we'd like to rent it for five weeks. He said, "That will be sixty dollars American. (Fifty dollars was for the owners, ten dollars went, of course, to Pako.)

We couldn't believe our good fortune. And when Pako found a woman and her son to shop, cook and clean for us at five dollars a week plus money to buy food, we were twice blest. (In order not to hurt their feelings when we'd talk about them in their presence we referred to them as Mickey Mouse and Donald Duck. They had the last laugh, however. The son was allowed to take from us whatever trinkets we'd leave out while he made up our rooms.)

Before I continue I need to refer back to our American friend in the taberna. He proved to be Doctor Paul Fussel, a junior professor at Rutgers. Paul later became head of the English Department there and was on sabbatical in Spain. He was a clever, sarcastic, humorous academic who was later to become famous for his essays in various New York City magazines and journals. One of his books, *Bad*, depicting all the things he found odious about Americans and their culture, is a classic. His cynicism over the body academe in which he found himself was evident even then.

Our days at the villa were all about the same. We'd get up around nine or ten, have breakfast, then study until lunch at two. Some of my Canadian friends were studying for their Roman Civil Law exams to be given when they returned to University. I was working on my Master's thesis which was to be sent back to my seminary in the United States for approval. (I still remember the title: *James Martineau: A Psychological and Existential Study* typed on a tiny portable typewriter.) I am sure to this day that John's agreeing to proofread it went a long way toward making it acceptable to the faculty back home. John later was to become Ambassador to Egypt for the Canadian government. (I also forgot to mention that Chris came to us from South Africa.)

After lunch we'd have our siestas then gather in the garden for wine and talk. This proved most enjoyable. Since we were able to purchase white and red wine produced locally for two dollars a bottle. (They were Nebuchadnezzars holding thirty-three bottles each and would arrive each week on a burro led by a young boy.)

One of my favorite pastimes was playing a game my friends called Botticelli – a sort of beefed-up version of Twenty Questions. If you were it, you'd choose a figure, either fictional or real, and you would give the players an indication of who you were not. For instance, if you chose to be General Douglas MacArthur you would begin the game saying, "I am not Viscount Montgomery." Then, in order to ask a direct question about who you were, they would have to stump you with a fact about some other figure whose name began with the same letter M.

Sholto and I were at the beach one day. I remember getting caught in a riptide and was nearly in panic until Sholto noticed my plight and started toward the water. Mercifully, I caught the right wave and got up and over the rip and in to the beach. While we were sitting there enjoying the sights, the beautiful wreck of a Moorish castle down the beach, the drying fish nets and small skiffs, two beautiful women came along. We greeted them with the usual "*Buenos dias,*" and they sort of giggled and hid their smiles. We asked if we might call on them. They said their duenna would allow it but that she must be there, too. I don't remember if we were able to call upon them but I do remember the strict rules young women had to observe when young men courted them. (On our trek up the mountain across from the village, Sholto and I joined in singing "Matilda" – only we substituted the name of one of the beautiful maidens we had met the day before.)

On another occasion, our friend Ken Lysyk (who later was to become a Supreme Court judge for the Province of British Columbia) had us all stumped playing Botticelli with his historical figure. Through painful questioning we had found that his chosen figure was the 1956 Champion Crow Shooter for Canada. When we finally, reluctantly, gave up, he spread his hands as if to say he couldn't understand how we could have missed it and said, "Frank Cosgrove." We were so put out with him for assuming we should know this bit of trivia that we gave strong consideration into throwing him into the nearby surf, fully clothed.

One day Sholto and I crossed the highway and hiked north to the nearby foothills. We had heard there was a village up the way and made it our destination. It proved to be a wonderful walk and the wine was just as good at the village taberna as the wine we missed back at the villa. And it was in that village (whose name was Las Yuccas, if memory serves) that the Rockport artist, William James Flynn, had done a painting of an antique door which became our possession thirty years later!

On one occasion Ken Lysyk and I took the bus into Malaga to change British pounds for American dollars. While we were there we learned that the annual Easter festival was going on. We found the city square where the parade was to pass. There was a reviewing stand for the usual public figures like the mayor and his entourage. Ken told me to follow him. Taking out his student pass with his picture on it, he showed the guard and told him we were members of the press. I had mine as well. The guard directed us to a seat near the mayor and it was from there that we watched a parade of huge floats pass. The floats were centered around the various saints being celebrated, the largest of which was that of the Virgin Mary. It consisted of five huge logs over a hundred feet each with the float supported on them and the statue of Mary. It was carried down the way by over a hundred men all swaying in unison, left, right, left, right and all humming the same tune. Quite a sight.

When we left the reviewing stand to find a place to change our money we happened on one of the numberless wine shops. The whole wall of the shop was lined with huge casks with different kinds of wine available. We both ordered some sherry and as we sat enjoying it a man came to our table with a tray. On it were these mahogany-colored bivalves with a brilliant red dot in the inner shell. We paid him some pesetas and he left the whole tray. They were delicious.

Changing the funds proved quite easy. A local bank did the trick. By this time the dinner hour had arrived. We ate at a fish restaurant and the fare was well-prepared. By this time it was nearly midnight. We knew that there was no bus service until the next morning. We aimlessly wandered along until we found ourselves down by the docks.

There was a small fishing boat tied to the dock. We got aboard and lay down on some coils of rope. Suddenly, there was this man with no legs who appeared almost out of nowhere. His body sat on a wooden platform with wheels and he pulled himself along by his hands. He told Ken, who understood Spanish, that the boat would be sailing for Africa the next morning early and that we should not stay there. Then he motioned for us to follow him. Soon we stood before a huge sliding door of a warehouse. With not a little effort the man managed to roll it back enough for us to enter. He indicated some tarpaulins on the dock. We took them and threw them on a great pile of bananas stored inside. The man left. We settled down and tried to sleep.

After a while I sensed some motion in the bananas. I flicked my lighter and, wonder of wonders, we had some new companions. They were tarantulas, dozens of them. Apparently, they, too, love bananas. And, they being there first, we took ourselves swiftly away. As I remember, we slept fitfully leaning against the outer walls of the warehouse until dawn when we caught the first bus back to Fuengirola.

We all returned to Oxford by various modes of transportation. Sholto owned a motorbike, a Wabo. He asked if I would like to share the return journey and I quickly agreed. I still remember marveling at the beautiful country sides through which we traveled. Here my memory is not so clear.

I do recall sleeping, with permission, in the barns of farmsteads and of learning how disgusted the French voters seemed to be with the incredible succession of unpopular premiers. I also recall our winding up at some "World's Fair" in either Brussels or the Netherlands where we made several trips around the candy exhibit stuffing ourselves as we had only enough money for our ticket on the ferry home. And there was a nice family who invited us to stay the night with them for dinner so their son could practice his English.

By now, gentle reader, you have probably grown weary of my meandering babble so I will close with a sincere dedication. My memories of that time in Spain continue to be vivid reminders of five friends with whom I shared our time away from school. Three years later, having finished my Master's degree, I was called to my first church. It was in Providence, Rhode Island and it was there that I met and married Lorna. Last August we celebrated forty-five years of marriage with our four children and six grandchildren.

My ministry took me to churches in Massachusetts, New Jersey, Texas (San Antonio and Houston) with Interim ministries in Florida, Santa Fe, New Mexico and back to Norwell, Massachusetts. It's been a real trip!

One after thought: our honeymoon took us to New York City where we were invited to stay the night with Sholto and his new bride. Since that time it is hard to believe that nearly fifty years have elapsed. I have not seen any of you, my friends, in person since that time. So here's to you Eric and to you, Ken and Niel. And, of course, another toast to John, Chris and Sholto as well.

You were kind to invite me to join you. Obviously I continue to remember our time together with great fondness and will continue to do so.

Allons!

Jan Vickery Knost
Harris-Manchester '58
Charlestown, Rhode Island – Winter, 2007

An Incredible Learning Experience

It was the spring of 1959. I had just been graduated Master in Divinity from Saint Lawrence University. The Department of Ministry of the Universalist Church of America had mandated that I spend a twelve-week session in chaplaincy training at a recognized hospital setting. Since my family was living in Malden, Massachusetts, I chose to go to the Boston State Mental Hospital in a program under the auspices of the Boston University Theological School.

What I anticipated was a wonderful opportunity to work with patients that would be grateful to me for all the support and assistance I would bring them and make them tied to me all their lives as they went from success to success. What I experienced was not the same as I anticipated. Oh, no, not at all!

The campus of BSMH (an institution that President Reagan's administration closed – but that's another tragic story) was a verdant campus of some one hundred acres (you can research it!) that was located in the Blue Hills section of South Boston.

We were a class of approximately thirty graduate students from various theological seminaries in the New England area. We would be housed on the campus, fed via the institutional facilities and would be reportable to our faculty of our sponsoring institution, Boston University. My roommate was a wonderful guy named Gerry Krick, a graduate of Harvard University Divinity School.

Our weekly schedule was the same: classes, individual meetings with mentors, work with our assigned patients, visits to the Medical Surgical building to witness actual surgical operations and what was to become an incredibly difficult session – our "interpersonal groups."

The classes were easy. We listened, took notes, studied the suggested chapters in books and took the examinations. Individual meetings with our supervisory mentors were a bit more difficult since each of them pushed us to explain why we were there and why we would want to enter such a difficult field. We were each assigned to work with a "chronic" mental patient. We were allowed this privilege since it was assumed that, given the refusal of the patient(s) to allude to reality any longer, we could do no harm to that patient since he/she was so far removed from reality that she/he could never be harmed by our sudden interference into their lives.

Interpersonal groups proved to be the most painful of all. We would sit in a small room – eight of us – accompanied by a faculty member and his/ her tape recorder. This, he/she would turn on at the beginning of each of our sessions. The explanation of a faculty presence was to make sure that we only remained on the topic and that that faculty member would, in no way, give opinions regarding conversation, one way or the other.

As the days d-r-a-g-g-e-d by during that "long, hot summer" in that little room, many participants began to get pissed off, not only at each other, but at our unwavering faculty person who remained neutral at every point. Gradually, guys (and we WERE all guys in 1959) began to waken to the task. At some point, person "A" would say, "I want to discuss 'B's' statement the other day when he said, '…'" Wow! That would bring it out. Different members of our group would be quick to say something. "Oh, right. What the hell did you mean by this or that…???"

Most of us, I suspect, learned that there was something far more significant regarding our "non-agenda" meetings. It was for us to become sensitive to the follies of living this life; of becoming sensitive to the reasons we had chosen our future professions and to wake us to our own weaknesses and strengths. Honestly, there was a time when I was heartbroken with what some of my colleagues voiced both to me and at me. But there were others when I felt strengthened and supported by their collegial affection. 'Nuff said.

Then there were our assignments to work with chronic patients. When the time came for the faculty and medical/psychiatric troops to feel we were ready for such a venture, all of us were given "a name." Mine was a man by the name of Hubert Knox, an Army veteran of the First World

War and he was an African-American. What followed in our work together I could neither have predicted nor imagined.

The lead psychiatrist sat me down in his office and said, "Jan, Hubert Knox was a shellshock victim in World War I. He has been this way since 1918. He is what we call a 'bedrock' patient. By that, I mean that I do not believe that there is any harm that can come to him with you working with him. But you can try. Perhaps there is some way you can bring him comfort."

With that I was politely dismissed to meet with my new "patient" the following day. When I was ushered into a small room off the ward where Hubert presumably lived, there he was. He was a black man, slightly overweight, sitting with his hands at his side and staring straight ahead as if there was no one there.

I took my seat in the chair opposite him. Silence. After a time, I said, "Good afternoon, Hubert. My name is Jan. I'm one of the chaplains here at the hospital. Is there anything you'd like to talk about?"

Nothing. No sound. No movement. Just staring eyes. This kept up in the second and third session with Hubert. Then I had a chance to speak with the head psychiatrist again. "I can't get anything out of him. He's just not speaking, and won't! I don't know what there is I can do."

The doctor thought for a few moments, nodding his head. Then, he looked at me and said, "Well, there is one kind of activity that has been used to reach chronic patients. It usually doesn't work but you could try it. Here's what you do. Get hold of a 'Nerf ball.' Do you know what a Nerf ball is?" I nodded. "Well, when you do, and at your next meeting, try taking the ball and bouncing it off his chest… over and over and over again. Sometimes… your effort may get a rise out of him. And when and if it happens, (and I don't hold out much hope that it will,) there's a split second of time when you may… I say 'may'… make contact with him. Anyway, it's a thought. Let me know how it goes."

Later that day I visited a Walgreen's on Blue Hill Avenue and purchased a shocking pink Nerf ball. I had it with me when my regular visit with Hubert arrived. I began as always, carrying on a one-sided conversation to which, as usual, there was no reply. Then I began to bounce the ball off his chest, catching it as it bounced back. I did this for the remainder of our time when the nurse came to accompany my patient back to the chronic ward. This process continued for the next two sessions. I felt like a dolt – that's a combination of a stupid person and a cruel tormentor. Then it happened.

As I was casually bouncing the ball on Hubert's chest, he suddenly, and but for a split second, looked up at me with what seemed to be rage in his eyes. Quickly I said, "Hubert, is there something you want? Is there something I can do to be of help?" He returned to his usual posture, slightly slumped, head down, no sound.

The next day it happened again. This time I got an answer. When I asked if there was something I could do to help, he mumbled, "Wanna' see my m…" "What was that?" I asked. "Wanna' see my momma…" The seemingly cruel process had clicked something deep inside him. At last there was something I could do. Something that would make me feel useful and not a callous fool dreaming of "being a minister."

The next day I didn't show up at any scheduled classes. I took leave of my residence and made my way to the Administration Building. There I got what I could of the meager information regarding my patient: birth, former place of residence, etc. I found his mother's listed address! When I arrived at the address given, a woman answered the door. I asked about Hubert Knox.

"Oh, yes, he and his mother used to live here but that was years ago. When he went to the hospital, she moved. You can ask the landlord if he has her address."

The landlord immediately gave me a lead. He said that the mother had, indeed, lived at his property but that after a few years she became unable to take care of herself and was placed in the State Hospital – a custom common in those days before Ronald Reagan closed all state mental hospitals. Was the custom wrong? Was Reagan wrong? Who knows?

What transpired was that I found Hubert Knox's mother had been a resident of the Boston State Mental Hospital for years. The two were never apprised of this fact. They lived on the same campus, about a half mile apart.

When I told the lead psychiatrist what I had found, it took only two days for the necessary paperwork to be borne through the hospital's bureaucracy.

Then, on a Wednesday afternoon, (and it was a Wednesday, I assure you,) I waited on a bench in the hospital park. A nurse came along with a patient in a wheelchair. It was Hubert's mother who'd been so close for so long without either of them knowing it. When she was wheeled up to him, the two of them knew each other immediately upon being told and they embraced.

It may have been the best thing I did as a minister… and I wasn't even ordained.

*   *   *

Addendum to "An Incredible Learning Experience"

During that same summer I spent in chaplaincy training at Boston State Mental Hospital, (before Reagan closed them all, leaving the patients on the streets!) I had another learning experience than the one with my chronic patient.

It occurred in the "twinkling of an eye" in the cafeteria. We were sliding our trays along, getting our powdered scrambled eggs and other such victuals. One of the patients who worked behind the counter was a rather friendly type who I only knew as "Harold."

As I came past him, he shoveled some of the egg mixture onto my plate. "Good morning, Harold, how are you?"

Quick as a flash he replied, "YOU DON'T MEAN THAT!"

It was like a punch to my solar plexus. I suddenly realized that I actually didn't mean it. I was only doing what I thought was customary and expected. But Harold, in typical fashion as a person who listens to what is being said all the time, had fastened on to a human truth. Most of the time we only say stuff. But to really follow through would be time-consuming and we are consumed with saving time, aren't we?

On a future occasion, the same thing happened as I was shaking hands with church members as they exited the sanctuary after services. As the Moderator of the congregation came by, I shook his hand and said, "How are you?"

He grabbed my hand, looked into my eyes and said, "Have you got twenty minutes?!"

Whoops! I'd done it again.

"Not Guilty"

The year was 1972. The event was a carefully planned anti-nuclear protest in the city of New York. The plan was for groups to "sit-in" in front of the embassies of the five nuclear nations. Our assignment was to locate in front of the Chinese embassy. There were about a hundred of us. Seven of the group were, like me, Unitarian Universalist ministers. We even wore our pulpit robes.

The affair was to be a peaceful "sit-in." Arrangements had been made with the NY constabulary for us to be about one hundred feet from the barriers in front of the embassy. We arrived around eight a.m. Folks sang peace songs. Speakers quoted poetry. There was a sense that, with the cooperation of the police, this action would succeed in waking folks to the nuclear threat worldwide. Then things took a different turn.

As yellow school buses arrived at the scene, a police officer with a bullhorn said, "I have been instructed to direct you all to disperse. If you refuse, you will be placed under arrest and transported to a courtroom. If you move on your own to the buses, you will be charged with a misdemeanor. If you have to be carried to the buses, you will be charged with a felony."

For quite some time, no one moved. This forced the hand of the police and we heard the same declaration again. Then, and oh, so slowly, demonstrators began to move toward the buses. My colleagues and I got up together and slowly went to one of the buses. Others refused. Teams of police came into the enclosure and began carrying folks to the buses, noting their names and descriptions.

What we couldn't have predicted was that the courtroom where we were to be arraigned was in Harlem, about a hundred blocks away. We later learned that this was to discourage the more activist demonstrators from returning to the scene a second time, although that proved a useless strategy for many who did.

We sat silently in the courtroom. When the judge entered, we were instructed to rise. He sat and instructed us to do so, too. Then, one by one, our names were read and we came before the bench and were asked how we pleaded. When my turn came, I stood before the judge, a little nervous, to be sure.

"Reverend Knost, you have been charged with a misdemeanor in not heeding to the instructions of the NYPD. Do you plead guilty or not guilty?"

Taking a deep breath, I looked the judge in the eye and said, "Your Honor, I plead NOT GUILTY by reason of government insanity."

The judge looked up, surprised. Then he said, "Your trial is set for next September. Dismissed."

Of course, the authorities, not wishing to give us another chance to voice our opinion in public, never held those court proceedings. The charges just… went away. We agreed that it had been a worthwhile venture. The die had been cast and later that summer over two million people marched the streets of New York with the same peaceful show of opposition to nuclear weapons.

"Not guilty by reason of government insanity." Kind of says it all, eh?

A Proud Dad Remembers

The year was 1973. For over a decade we spent our summers in Hingham, Massachusetts. It was a short walk from where we lived to the harbor where I kept *The Diet of Worms*, my ancient nineteen-foot Bristol. Once a year I'd take a friend fishing who'd lost a leg in the War. My son, Keith, would come along to assist. We would be fishing that day on Quincy Bay for flounder in the days before over-fishing ruined it.

As I navigated the circuitous channel out of harbor, we came upon a school of menhaden flashing their tails at us. I grabbed a rod rigged with a weighted treble hook and snagged one, putting it on our guest's line. Then I caught another and put it on Keith's rod. They were live-lining their "pogies" when suddenly Keith's reel "sang out." Weighing only eighty-five pounds, he had trouble "heading" the fish. Then, in no time, the fish was into his backing and I had to run up on it to save line.

It took Keith fifteen minutes to bring that fish to the boat. Me? I was trying to coach him, though nervous as a hog on ice. ("Keep your rod tip up! Point your rod at the fish," etc.) Keith kept his calm and reeled. Finally, we boated what proved to be the stripe bass pictured here. She weighed 49 lbs. 9 ozs. and was nearly as long as Keith was tall. Keith later received letters of commendation from Governor Francis Sargent of Massachusetts and Senator Ted Kennedy.

* * *

Three years ago on a bright sunny day, as Keith was driving to his next job in New Orleans, the steering failed in his car. It rolled eighty-five feet and crashed around a tree. Keith suffered a broken neck and spinal cord injuries. He lives in an assisted living facility in New Jersey now as a paraplegic. He has never lost his sense of humor or his ability to hope for stem cell research to someday make him walk again.

Dad's Recipe For "Clean Scrambled Eggs"

Ingredients:
  6 jumbo sized free-range chicken eggs
  2 tbsp. heavy cream
  1 tbsp. butter

Whip the eggs thoroughly and add the heavy cream.

Melt butter in a round-sided sauté pan.

When the butter bubbles, add the eggs.

Begin turning as the lower part of the mixture begins to cook.

Continue turning rapidly until the whole mélange is glistening.

It is most important that it be turned out of the pan before the eggs start to brown. This produces what children describe as that "brown icky" look.

Salt and pepper to taste.

Feeds – Oh, I dunno'. Depends on how much the kid(s) have grown.

Optional: You may add hand-grated cheddar to the mixture if acceptable to the recipients. Mine never did.

A LITTLE MYSTERY

It was my first day "on the job." Time? 1990. Place? Emerson Unitarian Church, Houston, Texas. Matter at hand? A tour of the buildings. I was accompanied by the church secretary of many years, a rather droll, mostly humorless woman of questionable age.

We had been through the church school buildings, and then Westwood Hall, named for the church's founding minister, and now were in the sanctuary. The former minister of twenty-five years, being a professed Unitarian Christian by the name of Schulman, preferred that all the various accoutrements of the church be referred to in Christian terms. Thus, the pulpit, the lectern, the altar, the chancel. etc., etc.

At the rear of the sanctuary was a door to a dark little room. I opened it to discover a deep double sink made of soapstone. On the left wall was a large refrigerator meant, I supposed, to keep altar flowers fresh, delivered, as they usually were, on Saturdays.

It was a rather dingy room, to be sure. But I was cautioned to always refer to it as "the sacristy" or none of the older members would know what I was talking about.

As we were about to leave, I looked again at the refrigerator. There, for all to see, was a small plastic carton about six inches tall and five inches square. "What's this?" I asked.

"Don't really know," came the reply.

I took it down and opened it. In it, I rather shakily discovered, were the last remains of a human being burned to ashes in cremation... but no identification! I turned it over and over, even removing the heavy, clear plastic sack. Nothing. "Got to be someone's," I said.

"I'll take care of it," was the woman's only comment.

That was the last I ever saw of it and never asked again what transpired in my absence. A mystery unsolved... and it remains so.

You, gentle reader, will be happy to know that one of the first things I did was suggest a new usage for that room. Being in my "honeymoon" of beginning ministry, the leadership not only agreed with my plan, but found funding for it.

It is now, and has remained, a room for nursing mothers or parents with cranky babies to occupy and still hear the service on a small loudspeaker. The glass in the door was removed and one-way glass was put in its place. After all, some nursing mothers do have the right of privacy, right? I rest my case.

A LIVING EDITORIAL

UUA Trustees opened their April 23 – 25 Board meeting in Boston a day after a bomb explosion in a courthouse sent a score of people to hospitals in this city wracked by violence engendered by reactions to court-ordered busing to enforce school desegregation.

Trustees interrupted their first-day session to enable those who wished – and most did – to participate in a Procession Against Violence called by Boston's mayor and endorsed by Massachusetts' governor, the NAACP and other groups

The suggestion to recess for the procession came from UUA President Robert Nelson West, who said participation by UUs would be a "visible statement against violence in this city where we have had our headquarters for 150 years."

The Rev. Jan Vickery Knost of Dedham, Massachusetts Bay District trustee, who moved the recess, had earlier opened the Board of Trustees' session with the following prayer.

The Board's actions and the prayer stand as our mid-May editorial.

- UU WORLD, May 15, 1978

Let us pray:
O Thou Who art forever with us in these fleeting years of life,
We stop to ponder the questions unanswered in our hearts again.
In this beautiful springtime of crocuses and daffodils,
When the spirit of new life lifts our eyes skyward for the hope reborn,
The vacuum of our petulant human nature stirs in our midst,
Yea, in this great city again.
We would be one humanity amidst the violence and self-hate around us,
And with the insanity of the mob screaming unreasoned vengeance,
We remember how our great religious heritage of love and justice

42

Has never failed to speak to unreasoned power.
Our joined hands around this table symbolize the unity of purpose
Re-enkindled here each time we meet – and through every church,
Every household and human heart to make us one.
Direct our minds to reason, our lips to speak the truth in gentleness,
Our steps to follow where the conscience leads.
In the name of all that's holy in the mind and heart of all humanity,
We pray.
Amen.

"Moonlighting"

Shortly after beginning a ministry in Summit, New Jersey, my wife and I suddenly found ourselves with our two eldest children out of high school and on to college. It was worrisome having two kids in college at the same time. But, as most parents do, we were determined to manage. What to do?

Unitarian weddings are few and far-between. Nevertheless, I was a minister and had legal authority to perform nuptials. So in an effort to underwrite tuition costs, we placed a $600 ad in the *Yellow Pages*. It read simply:

The Rev. Jan Vickery Knost, B.S., M.Div.
Interfaith Weddings Performed
Telephone xxx-xxxx

Wow! It surely worked!

Slowly my ability to cross denominational and cultural lines by helping couples plan their weddings became known throughout the New Jersey wedding circuit. In fact, it worked so well that on one hot June Sunday alone, following the service at my church, I conducted six, back-to-back weddings starting at one p.m. and concluding the last one at eight that night. A lot of credit for this accomplishment goes to my daughter, Kristan. My back was out from a long-time sports injury from tournament volleyball. With her at the helm of our little VW Bug, we navigated the towns and countryside and weren't late even once.

The sites ran from a mansion in Morristown, to a third floor tenement in Orange, to a rented church, private homes and even a corral with barn, horses and TV personalities! At the last, the TV stars asked that I wear blue jeans and a blue work shirt. Not to worry.

Along the way I discovered an anomaly I had been seconding in signing all those wedding licenses. Halfway down the page, it was divided with a vertical line. On one side the words read: "Groom:" and "Occupation." On the other side the words read: "Bride:" and "Name of former husbands, if any." Realizing I had been going directly against a moral standing I had held for decades regarding the equality of women, I later called an emergency meeting of our Unitarian Universalists Ministers' New Jersey Chapter and brought it to their attention. They marveled that not one of them had caught this irregularity either.

We composed a letter which we all signed and posted it to the Secretary of State in Trenton, New Jersey. It took a little time, but soon, this error was corrected and I continued doing weddings with a littler clearer conscience. I have often wondered how long the State of New Jersey would have continued with a marriage license containing that untimely request. Knowing the way state government bureaucracies grind on, it could have continued to this day.

Allons! To the trenches! And fight the good fight!

But back to my "moonlighting" days. Kristan and I arrived home from that six-wedding marathon and I handed my beloved wife, Lorna, checks and cash amounting to $900 and said, very simply. "Here, love. Put this toward the college tuition."

Looking back, I can honestly say that not once did my extra work in the matrimonial vineyard ever compromise my sixty-hour work week for my congregation. It was something we did to ensure a future for our children as I'm sure those of you in similar circumstances have forged ways for you own.

But six weddings in a single day! I've never heard of another colleague who topped that one.

ANOTHER KIND OF MOTHER'S DAY TALE

It was nearly dusk. I was sitting in the woods next to a small pond waiting for a hatch to begin. Maybe this would be the day a trout would rise. The woods were still. All of a sudden a duck appeared, quacking away. Then, behind her, came six little ducklings, chirping, doing quick circles, but staying mostly in line. They were about to head across the pond when the mother duck began to quack more quickly. She turned toward the underbrush again and the ducklings followed her.

Above us I heard the "*skreee*" of a predator. Looking up, I saw an osprey circling the pond. The mother duck became more animated, paddling furiously, quacking to her brood. Then, without warning, the hawk folded its wings and dropped toward the surface of the water, the ducklings its target.

Just as quickly, the mother duck jumped from the water, her wings beating furiously, and positioned herself straight up on a collision course with the diving fish hawk. In seconds, the hawk saw this and bore off to the side. The duck splashed back to the surface and rejoined her family.

What seemed just moments passed, the hawk calling out, circling again. Then, in graceful, but malevolent manner, it folded its wings again and dropped toward the water. In like manner, the mother of her babies jumped again from the surface in the same straight suicidal leap at the diving bird. The hawk turned away again.

I don't remember how long this scenario played out. Two or three times more at least. Then the hawk gave up, giving vent to its cries as it flew over the trees to find a new target. The mother circled her young and began quacking in that low, regular beat of assurance that they were safe again. The little family disappeared into the bushes and all was still.

Mothers come in all sizes and shapes. They hold one characteristic in common. There is nothing they will not do, no heights they will not climb, no enemy they will not face to protect their offspring. I sat for another hour, amazed, inspired, in gratitude for my own Mom, though dead these many years. Mothers be praised!

A Governor's Visit

It was the advent of the onset of feminism – and especially in New England. I had awakened to the call in my home. Realizing my newly constituted role as a husband and as father of four growing children, I finally said to my beloved partner, "Hey, I know now what this all means. Now can you let me know what there is that I need to do? Let me know. What is it?"

Very simply, my Lorna said, "Hey, bub... if it's a job that needs doing, then DO IT!"

From then on I never needed a word or deed of coaxing.

In the spirit of urging the issues of feminism on, we planned a series of feminist weekends to be held at the church. We invited well-known feminist speakers to lead seminars on various topics and to top it all off I invited Francis Sargent, governor of the Commonwealth of Massachusetts to be the Sunday morning speaker on the third weekend of the series.

All went well, all through the various lectures, discussions and other events. The governor was especially gracious in his praise of the new feminist movement as he took the pulpit.

As the final hymn was beginning, I turned to Governor Sargent and said, "Your Honor, I hope you will be careful as you dismount the stairs from the pulpit here as we leave for the benediction at the rear of the church."

He, remembering the 1820 *Dedham* court decision that gave the right of all churches to hold property, replied, "It would be an interesting court case, wouldn't it?"

I have never forgotten that moment. And what a grand person "Frannie" Sargent was, indeed.

A Summer Idyll

It was summer and one of the many years we spent in New England. We were again "house-sitting" an ancient (1728) home near the harbor in Hingham, Massachusetts. Each morning was the same, yet now it was somehow different. We'd arrived at the docks and already there would be the quiet, early-morning "busy-ness" so typical in the predawn. The captains always had the engines to their Nova Scotian lobster boats chugging away in neutral – the air heavy with the smell of diesel fuel as they warmed up for the day ahead.

Loading the boat was easy – or difficult – depending on the tide. There is a nine to twelve foot tidal fall in Boston Harbor. When low the fifty-five gallon drums of bait must be lowered by block and tackle to the boat deck. Care had to be taken lest one let the rope slip and throw the load out of balance. The content of a fifty-five gallon drum of "fish-frames" was something to behold when spread over a boat's deck surface. Also, one needed to be wary of one's footing so as not to be dragged over, should the barrel fall into the water. I always seemed to get the job of loading those barrels.

Loaded up, we donned our "slicker" aprons scrubbed clean as a whistle from the previous day's labors. We then began to stretch the plastic bait bags for filling. We worked in the upraised stern. The Nova Scotian hull has no gunwale in the stern since the lobsters traps need "catapulting" from the back of the boat when set. Footing was always persnickety. And so, as the *Honey II* slid out of harbor, we began filling the 350 bait bags. "Bait big today," came the call from the captain, "we're leavin' these down 'til Saturday."

As we worked, we'd watch the passing docks, inlets, islands and the morning commuter boat. It would always pass us in the channel, its thirty knot-per-hour wake building with the crescendo of its huge twin engines. Occasionally we'd see Mark's pretty wife, Debbie, waving at us from the deck, her red hair blowing in the breeze. She'd be on her way to work in downtown Boston. We'd wave quickly and return to our work. The bait bags had to be finished before we reached our first line of traps, called a "trawl." The task of baiting is onerous when one considers the slippery deck, the pitching of the boat and the smell of the bait, called "gurry." I never seemed to mind it, thought, and the reason was quite simple.

We were "out there" again. We were away from shore on the water in beautiful Boston Harbor which, once more, sort of "belonged to us." We'd pass through the narrow channel between the end of Hull, Massachusetts and Peddocks Island – called "Hell Gut" – continue by historic Fort Warren and George's Island. We'd run out to Boston Lighthouse to the outer Brewster Islands. We were out there again and we were free.

Would it be a good day or a "bust"? A good day would be one in which we'd average a legal-sized lobster per trap. A "bust" would be quickly realized as the captain would begin, more and more, to offer his shrill profanities as each trawl was hauled producing little but hard work.

I know it sounds kind of selfish, but I didn't much care. I had little invested in the venture except a few traps and the exercise was good. I <u>was</u> concerned that Mark have a good catch, but beyond that, just being out there was enough. No telephones, no crises but plenty of time to think, wonder and to dream.

There is a monotony in pulling a line of twenty-five traps attached to one line. It is all but hypnotic. The captain would line up the boat with the first colorful "pot markers." One of us would lean over the gunwale with the boathook and haul the line aboard. The captain would put the boat in neutral, give a wind of the line around the hauler wheel and turn on the hauler engine. Lobstermen call the hauler a "slave." The long, lazy grind of its power would drone in our ears, stopping, starting, getting jammed.

After a hundred feet or so the first trap would come bursting out of the water. Usually it was draped with beautiful, sleek glistening chestnut-brown kelp weed, some leaves as long as thirty feet. We'd cut this away and then, "A winnah! A winnah," the captain would exclaim as he peered through the slats of the trap at a two or three-pounder, its tail slapping the air.

The captain would slide the trap along the foot-wide gunwale to Mark who'd open it, reach in and grab the keeper-lobsters. These he would throw in the banding box for later measuring. He'd then begin throwing the "shorts" overboard as well as the numberless crabs. He'd pull out the bait bag, now filled with only fish bones, slap it on the side of the boat to empty it and grab a full one. This he would place in the "kitchen" portion of the trap then close and secure the lid and slide the trap along to me. I would pick it up and carry it to its eventual launching position taking care to shove the line out of the way. (Line in lobster terms is called "pot wrap," pronounced "pot wop" by New Englanders.) The whole process – trap up, trap emptied, trap baited, trap placed – took less than a minute. And you had to be quick – there was another trap breaching the surface.

A half-hour average per trawl was excellent time, provided there were no snags or cut-offs. It was backbreaking work since there was no way of slacking once the first trap was aboard. With a wet deck, vigilance was a mandate. More than once launching has a lobsterman been dragged overboard and down to his death by a snagged line around an ankle.

We'd rest in between trawls, wolfing down a bit of lunch, reading the latest Red Sox loss or simply sitting, straddling the side gunwale, our boots gliding in and out of the wake as we proceeded to the next marker. The waves of greeting to other boats were simple, perfunctory, familiar. There is not a lot of trust among fishermen when one does it to support a family. And there was less time for idle chit-chat. This was the big leagues with boats working 400 or more traps each day, 800 – 1200 in a week!

Nevertheless, the swooping gulls never failed to amaze with their flight aerobatics, their keen eyes which could see a bit of bait slip overboard from as far as a quarter mile away. Or one could close the eyes and listen to their "laughing" comic cries, complaining, probably, of empty bellies. It was an ever-changing vista of happenings, always beautiful, surging with peace, power and possibility.

For me, one familiar with my professional calling; there was religion out there "in-between." A calmness always seemed to descend upon me no matter the weather – calm, foggy, windy or sun-drenched. Its essence was in the regularity of our labors, the harvesting and performing the ordinary, the necessary, almost in obeisance to Neptune or Poseidon and the wonders of the deep.

Would that one's life could take on such a rhythm! Would that one's attention to the gift of simply being alive could be as constant. The insights came so serendipitously aboard that craft. They were so subtle yet profound. I returned each day, tired and sore, with bleeding hands and fingers from the tiny puncture wounds received in being careless as I banded the lobsters for market. And yet, during those returns to harbor I always felt more complete knowing there had been a job well done.

Skimming over the water with the sun past its zenith I would feel a sense of gratitude at having been counted as one with this strange breed of sea creatures called lobstermen. Accepted. Trusted. One with them.

There have been other times.

There have been other remarkable, even extraordinary times.

But that brief summer was sort of special, don't you know? Its daily rhythm reached inside to tell me that life was good.

Herman Melville had been so right in choosing the Sea as his symbol of God.

A rhythm – a rhythm and a balance – so necessary was mine. It is so often overlooked or taken for granted. It is our Being as we are enchanted and enhanced by idylls of experience. It was a rare and valuable time for me and I understood, just a little more, what life is all about.

As each day comes, as we do the necessary, we often find places in our life history to which we can return that were not so ordinary. In that reverie the heart pumps just a bit faster, one's breathing deepens and we know a sense of peace… and maybe even… God.

So be it.

- Tarpon Springs, Florida, 1998

"Bible People"

The phone on my desk rings. "Hello."

"Yes, Reverend, this is John Smith at the funeral home. We've got a situation here. I hope you can help us out. There's been a death but the family of the deceased won't cooperate in planning his service. They're all estranged from him."

"Why?"

"Well… I think you'll figure that out once you get here. Can you spare some time this morning?"

"Well, yes. I have a couple of things to get done first, then I'll drop by."

Mid-morning. I tell the church secretary that I'll be at the funeral home if something comes up. I give her the number. It takes three minutes in our small town for me to get there. The receptionist ushers me into the director's office. There are two men seated there, the director behind his desk and a man in early fifties in the chair opposite. We're introduced.

The director says, "You see, Reverend, the situation is this. The family hasn't spoken to their son in years. I think it's a religious thing but I'm not sure. Mister Jones here might clear things up."

My new acquaintance tries to settle more comfortably in his seat. He clears his throat, seeming reluctant to speak.

The director prompts, "Go ahead, Mister Jones. The minister is an understanding professional. I've worked with him quite often."

"Well, sir, you see, it's like this. Bill and I have been what you might call partners for nearly fifteen years. We've lived in the same apartment, paid our bills and kept our jobs. But Bill's family is unable to accept our… er… friendship. They think of themselves as devout Christians. They think both of us are sinners because the Bible is the word of God. They also claim it was me who, as they put it, "stole their son.""

There is a long uncomfortable pause. I take care to make a reply that will be both reassuring and comforting. Obviously, Jones was in deep grief over his loss. Thinking back, I now realize, too, that I was witnessing only the tip of what, in years to come, would be an iceberg of homophobia across our great nation. So I answer him, "One of the privileges of serving a liberal congregation is that I am free to assist families in planning various services of passage: weddings, child dedications, and most certainly memorial services. I have designed a handbook that I can get to you. It is comprised of readings, poetry, prayers and other elements that can be put together to celebrate Bill's life. Would you be able to spend some time with that handbook and then get back to me?"

The director seemed instantly relieved. The stress and tension that had been present was suddenly gone.

"Yes, that will be most helpful. Could you do the service for Bill here this coming Saturday?"

"Of course."

The day arrived. Our carefully planned service was typed up and lay open on the lectern before me. On one side of the room sat Bill's partner. Across the aisle sat several people, all of whom, I assumed, were members of Bill's family. I began the service and as I read on, the grief that Bill's partner had so successfully hidden suddenly broke forth. At first it was a sniffle. Then it was a catch of breath. Then it was a keening sound in his throat and then, total tears and sobs. And so it continued.

So, too, did the neutral, passive, frowning, staring faces of the family. Not a sound. Looking straight ahead and trying to ignore the sadness in the room, they almost sighed that the event would soon be over.

I have dedicated my life to serving the cause of religious freedom and the heavy, endless task of "bringing comfort to the afflicted and to afflict the comfortable." But I shall never forget the rising outrage that I felt as I regarded those unfeeling, hypocritical and loveless "Christians."

Let us grieve for our brothers and sisters who love each other, believe in each other and who are of the same sex and tragically, but realistically, are hated for their efforts.

And they call themselves "Bible people?" Balderdash!

UP FROM 800 FEET!

Garibaldi, Oregon
May, 2004

The captain's daughter was also first mate of our charter. As I let the forty ounce, round sinker to the bottom she came over, examined my reel and said cheerfully, "Great! You're about halfway there!"

The reel was very large and had been totally filled with braided line when I began. It had already been over a minute since I released the clutch. Nervously, I asked, "Just how deep is it here?"

"Oh, about 800 feet," she said. "Just keep it smooth. You'll get there soon."

Eight hundred feet may be a long way down but it's certainly a lot longer reeling up! With a fish on one's line, in this case, about a forty-five pound halibut, it's a lot harder than just the weight itself because the fish will stay at a level. The weight just wants to observe the laws of gravity and fall again. So it was on a day last month.

We had gone to visit my wife's sister and husband in Salem, Oregon. He laid on a charter trip for the two of us out of the coastal town of Garibaldi. The state only allows charters and private boat owners three days a year to catch halibut and that's it – another triumph of our nation's regulatory commissions. Everyone, including captain and mate, returned with his or her limit of one fish.

And yet, gentle reader, let's be honest. Standing on a pitching deck with six-foot seas and swells to boot is no picnic when you're trying to get a fish weighing more than one of my grandchildren off the bottom. It's just plain… work! Several of the younger customers were called into service a number of times, the old muscles of sailors such as yours truly burning with folic acid. On more than one occasion, spontaneous cheering sections urged the struggling angler up from the depths to new heights. So it continued throughout the morning.

Next May, you may want to visit the beautiful Oregon coastline and avail yourself of one of these: "once-in-a-lifetime" trips to an area twenty-eight miles out. I can attest to its challenge and the excitement of it all. And the memory will last a lifetime… which is surely enough for this old duffer!

- Jan Vickery Knost, "Fisher of Men" Retired to Charleston, Rhode Island

MINISTRY – THE OCCASIONAL "MIASMAL SWAMP"

During our years in San Antonio, I was using recycled paper on which to type my weekly sermons. One Sunday, we were singing the hymn that comes just before the sermon. Singing along with the congregation, I suddenly realized that a tickle was starting in my throat. Not taking my eyes off the words of the hymn, I nonchalantly reached toward the shelf mounted under the pulpit. As I did, I was horrified to hear the glass tip over, water running everywhere!

When I pulled my manuscript up from that mess, I discovered, that those recycled pages had quickly melded together into what I can only describe as papier-mâché.

We sang the "Amen". I signaled for the congregation to be seated. Then, as if nothing was at all wrong, I began to peel each sheet from the messy mass. Of course the water had kind of faded what was typed and I had to guess what it was that I was sharing without giving the slightest indication of my plight.

Somewhere there's a parishioner from that church there in San Antonio who still wonders just what in hell the preacher was talking about in his sermon that day. Still, no one said a word when I shook their hands as they headed to "drink the holy beverage" at coffee hour. Maybe they were just too kind. I don't know.

At any rate, there was no way on God's green earth that yours truly was gonna' say a word about it. Sheesh!

Taking the High Road

Webster defines the word sportsman as "One who pursues field sports, especially hunting and fishing." Indeed. There is no doubt that our fields and streams are made better by such organizations as Trout Unlimited and Ducks Unlimited. The various fishing clubs whose memberships make up the Rhode Island Salt Water Fishing Association all try to impress on their members the importance of fair play and good conduct. Unfortunately, this is not always the case. Here are some examples, past and present.

Years ago the great Chesapeake Bay was almost empty of striped bass. Commercial trawlers hauled in thousands of tons of the migratory species. (It has been alleged that one net caught one weighing in excess of 125 lbs.) Such over-fishing has its inevitable result. Waters starved of fish for all to enjoy. It's happened, too, in a bay south of Boston where flounder were the staple for decades. Then busloads of New Yorkers came. They would arrive at eight a.m.; rent all the craft available, purchase a gross of sea worms and fill plastic garbage barrels with their take. Afterwards, off to New York again. Three summers of this ruined a wonderful fishery.

Recently we heard of a group of Rhode Island "sportsmen" who followed the stocking truck to a local trout impoundment. No sooner had the fish been released into the water than the "fishermen" began to cast, dragging the naïve fish out before they ever had a chance to relocate themselves. When asked if this was sporting behavior, one "sporting type" was said to have replied, "They all taste the same when you cook them in a frying pan." How sad.

The majority of folks no doubt show a lot of respect for the right of all sportsmen to enjoy this state's excellent stocking program. Given the kind of behavior previously mentioned though, it would not be long before such antics would "kill the fish that laid the golden egg sacs." How about the High Road of sportsmanship instead?

[*This article appeared in a local paper anonymously.* – JVK]

WEDDING STORIES

Through the years the weddings at which I officiated number in the hundred, perhaps even more. Here are a few scenarios in which I found myself.

During a July wedding on an incredibly hot day when the AC in the wedding mill wasn't doing its job, one of the groomsmen fainted. I had been told that he ignored my advice at the rehearsal to avoid "partying it up" too much the evening before. Not long after I had begun the service I noticed him begin to sway forward and back, forward and back. Then, on about the third round, he toppled backwards to the carpet. Two of the other groomsmen got some ice water, helped him into a chair and we continued the service to the end. The poor guy just sat there, staring into space, shaking his head over and over.

Then there was the time that the parents of the groom somehow got lost on their way to the event. So the best man went to find them. After nearly an hour, he called the manager of the restaurant to say he, too, was lost. With the happy agreement of the rest of the party and guests, we began the service. Near the end, first the parents, then the best man, sheepishly made their way to the front near the bride and groom. "Sorry, folks," was the meek announcement from the father of the groom… and that was that.

On another occasion (and this one was told to me by a wedding photographer), when all the wedding party had been introduced at the reception and had entered as couples, then came the explanation, "And, ladies and gentlemen, here they are for the very first time as Mr. and Mrs. John Smith!" Down the aisle came the happy couple. The groom was very tall. As they walked under the rather low hanging chandelier he kind of ducked, but didn't bend far enough and the "tentacles" of that glass lighting grabbed his toupee as he walked right out from under it. The hairpiece hung there, like a little bird, as the audience gasped and held back their laughter. Blushing, the groom quietly retrieved his possession and joined his partner.

One day I had to do a wedding in a tenement in a very tough part of the city. So tough it was that there were three groomsmen waiting on the sidewalk to accompany to the third floor flat where the wedding was to take place. They were a poor couple. But they were rich in love and imagination. When it came time to exchange rings, they did something beautiful. Instead of a ring, the bride had created a silver bracelet engraved with words of love to her husband. Also rejecting the expense of a ring, the groom, a starving musician, played on his guitar and sang a love song he had composed for his bride. It was a time of happy tears for all in that cramped space. But a moment one would never forget.

In this scene, the groom and best man had been painting houses and saving their money – the groom to pay for his share of the wedding and the best men to help with his college tuition. When I asked the best man to give the groom the ring for the bride, he reached into his tuxedo jacket pocket and pulled out a brand new paintbrush – which he handed to the groom. The groom looked at it, looked at me, looked at his friend then back at the paintbrush and said, very simply, "Whaaaaa???"

The photographer introduced herself to me at the rehearsal. I went through the litany of cautions I did at every rehearsal, asking her to use available light, not flashes and to be as "invisible" as possible during the actual ceremony. She nodded her head as if she'd heard it all before, which, I suspect, she had. Then came the day of the ceremony. Now this person was, to put it mildly, quite overweight. Nevertheless, she chose to show up in a shocking pink upper draping. Accompanying her was a camera on a rolling tripod. When the wedding march began she not only stood in the center aisle like some great pink battleship, but she actually backed down the aisle in front of each approaching groom, groomsmen, bridesmaid and finally the bride and her father! Each time she would squeakily push the tripod to the rear of the aisle and do it again. When the service was over, I informed her that what she had done was quite unprofessional and that I would do my best to make sure all my colleagues were aware of her affronts to good taste. Sheesh!

At a wedding reception held in a rather rococo "palace" I was standing with the father of the bride, a rather large person who towered over me in height. (I'm 6'2".) His name was Vinnie. "Hey, Reverend," he said.

"Yes, Vinnie?"

"Ya dune a good job. Here." With that he took out a four-inch roll of bills, peeled off the outside one – a hundred dollar bill – and proceeded to push it into my suit jacket pocket.

"No, Vinnie. That's okay. The kids already paid me."

"Naw, just keep it as somethin' extra. Buy your little woman something with it."

Not wanting to pursue the matter any further for fear of screwing up, I said, probably more to make sounds than with any purpose in mind, "Well, thank you. Er… ummm… what business are you in, Vinnie?"

"Garbage," came the reply.

This in a state where the Mafia controls trash collections statewide… and I realized that I had officiated at a Cosa Nostra wedding. Gee, that was close!

Here we go again. A couple who were not church members made an appointment to ask if I would help them plan their wedding. Their caveat was that it was to be performed in a Mexican restaurant. No problem. As long as the setting was quiet. So we did. The day arrived. I was there, robe in hand. The maitre d' took me to a private room. I changed. I came out at the appointed time. The couple was there. I stood there, ready to begin the service. Suddenly, lights came on. We were being photographed by video cameras. An "Elvis impersonator" appeared. He began to sing, "Love me tender, love me true…" On it went. When he finished, the groom nodded to me to begin. So I did. Unknowingly and to my horror, I found that the service, complete with Elvis, was being recorded by a local TV station for the eleven o'clock news! I drove home in anger, feeling I'd been "hornswoggled" by the couple. Then I prayed, asking that the powers that be assist me by having every one of my board members asleep when the news came on. No one ever mentioned it but I felt such a fool.

A Japanese couple asked me to perform a wedding at the Four Seasons Hotel. It was to be a private affair with fifty guests followed by a reception for over three hundred. They were content with letting me decide what the service would be like and didn't show a bit of concern. The day came,

I arrived, the couple joined me with their special guests in a private room. I did the service then proceeded to the reception. When I approached the best man to ask for the wedding license, he played dumb. Assuming language was the problem, I went to the maid of honor. She smiled, shook her head and said, "Oh, sir... they are not being married by you. They plan to be married back in Tokyo by a Shinto priest. They just wanted to honor their American friends with (how shall I say) 'the semblance' of a service. You don't need to worry about signing any kind of license." With that and a harmless giggle, she turned and went back to the reception. I always wondered whether I had done anything wrong...

Then there was the time I was standing in a rather Byzantine garden with the groom and best man. The guests were all in their seats on the green and perfect lawn. The music started and in came the beautiful bridesmaids, one at a time. Finally, as the bride approached holding tightly to her father's arm, it happened. I can still hear the screams. Suddenly, the underground watering system came on under the guests' chairs. What I witnessed was truly "Bedlam!" Finally, as in all things happy, order was restored. The women guests stopped muttering imprecations under their breaths and the service began. I never had the fortitude to ask the manager of that wedding mill what happened insurance-wise following the scene.

Oh, then there was one story I heard from that same photographer. I have only to say that it had to be apocryphal since it is hard to believe it really happened. But here goes. The rector of the local Episcopal church was conducting the service. He came to the part in the ceremony where he asked, "If any of you know why this couple may not lawfully be joined together, speak now, or forever hold your peace." With that, the groom stepped up to the side of the minister, turned, looked at the best man and the bride and said, "He (pointing to the best man) has been sleeping with her (indicating the bride). Have a nice party!" And with that he strode down the center aisle and out of the church. I can only marvel at such rude, inappropriate but honest courage and wonder if the father of the bride ever got over it.

In conclusion let me say that, notwithstanding these many strange, often humorous and sometimes painful peccadilloes, it has been my pleasure and privilege to have performed scores of weddings that were beautiful and for which I received praises, I probably don't deserve, for my professional manner. But you, dear reader, have read of some of the others that gave me a bit of a concern and most certainly, in recalling them, a smile, a chuckle and sometimes even a loud guffaw!

Blest be.

P.S. Then there was the time I performed a wedding for the son of a church member in Kerrville, Texas. It was on the day before the annual folk festival was to begin – an event attracting thousands each year. The place where the service was to be held was called "Chapel Hill" and was a small clearing in the woods with crude wooden benches, a cross nailed to a tree and a roughly fashioned podium. The time was past when the ceremony was to begin so I asked the bride waiting next to me where the groom had gone. She said, "Oh, he's over the hill with the groomsmen doing their Texas traditional 'thingy.'" I walked over to the edge and there they were, six guys in a circle. They were passing around a bottle of whiskey, each one in turn taking a pull and saying a few words. When it finally came to the groom he looked at me, took the last swig and said to his friends, "Okay, guys, let's do this." And with that they all trooped up to the front to await the beginning of the service. I began. When I read Paul's Letter to the Corinthians, someone in the audience whispered loud enough for all to hear, "Oh, Wow! Where'd he get that? It was neat." Then when I got to the prayer of blessing for the couple and said, finally, "Amen," it happened. Never before had I ever received applause for a prayer. But, then again, these were folk people and didn't do much in the way of church stuff.

LORNA SMITH KNOST

(b. January 15th, 1943, Providence, Rhode Island)

A TRIBUTE

This all started in my mind with a simple phone call. "Okay. When I'm at the Stop and Shop I thought I'd get a few artichokes for tonight."

"Oh, no. Jana's allergic to them."

Simple conversation. Simple thought. But it goes much deeper than that. The person with whom I spoke was my beloved wife and partner of over fifty years. And in an instant, she revealed to me the depth of her excellence as a wife and mother.

Not only that, she has been a trusted confidante for near half a century in times when judgment, reason and clear thinking have been necessary for us to survive thinking ahead for our family ship of state.

Lorna was so quiet and so lovely and so ever-inducing of my attention when I met her. She knew who she was and did not hesitate to let you know her feelings and her intent. We bonded immediately and I will never be able to ask her forgiveness enough for the night she pushed my little '59 VW Bug out of the snow to get her home from my apartment that wonderful night in 1960.

So it goes.

Our years together have been rich, full of joy and full of the welcome of four splendid children. Add to that the anticipation and then the celebration of the births of nine (that's 9!) grandchildren.

But the years "in-between" were classic. Can you imagine the numberless wonderful people we've welcomed into our home – the leaders of churches who we've trusted, and those not so? Can you think of a way to describe the fantastic travels we've done with kids and alone? To Europe and Great Britain, to Transylvania and across the United States? Boggles the mind to just recall.

Lorna's professional life was an incredible record. She started as a simple clerk in a department store, worked her way up to a model, all the while commuting from her family home to work and then to school and back. Not with a lot of help from home, to be sure.

She worked in a bank as a teller, preparing herself as a manager and finally heading up a staff of thirty in a bookstore with an inventory worth of over two million dollars. She also worked for Home Depot, winning a dozen or more "merit badges" to cut glass, wood, Formica and other customer needs. All this time she proved her fantastic sense of taste and style in the ways she made our home, whether parsonage or (Thank God!) our own home one of style, grace and beauty. There is no doubt that many who knew her talents would say that she missed her calling in not going the route of interior decorator. I agree.

But most of all she was a religious educator. She prepared herself for that track by taking a number of UUA designated weekend training sessions in over a dozen prescribed areas. And she was GOOD! She authored a junior high school curriculum about learning the various faiths whose model is still used in many UU churches today.

Her work in one church in the Southwest proved her excellence beyond all means. And the beat went on. When we moved to Houston, there was a church, not of her own denomination, who hired her to lead a church school of over 200 kids! The church still grieves her leaving and many members write her often to thank her for her leadership.

In concluding this missive I cannot but recall the constancy of Lorna's love and abiding counsel for her children. She is always there for them… no matter how long the phone call. And she remembers… remembers birthdays, anniversaries, anything celebrated.

We lie in bed each night and morning, this wonderful, beautiful lady and my humble self and I know that I sleep next to a champion, a strong bond to our children, and an incredible support to me both in my past profession and in my trying to stay alive. And I love her. Love her with constancy and with gratitude. For, after all is said and done, she is a giant of persons and… can you believe it… she is an angry… unforgiving… Democrat!!!

God, do I love that woman!

Jan Vickery Knost
Charlestown, Rhode Island
July 6th, 2011

A Memoir to a Better Era

This look at the past is dedicated to you, the 1952 graduating class of Peoria Central High School. Since I arrived in Peoria as a senior, I have always thought of you, my classmates, as "the class that took me in." Considering the warm memories I have of that year and of our times that followed when we gathered to remember, I will be eternally grateful.

Think back. Weren't they simpler days? Were we not the recipients of a land made stronger by its passage through the Great Depression? We were taught that it made one a better person by working hard. Our jobs as youngsters were simple, to be sure. We were "carry-out boys," babysitters, helpers who were paid little but learned much.

We'd haul scrap metal to the junkyard and sell it for a penny a pound. A nickel tip for carrying groceries to the customers' cars was a lot. Penny candy abounded and technology was decades away. Our country's flag had been protected through the pain of World War II and many of us longed to be old enough to fight. Our rooms were filled with model airplanes and ships. Gold Star Mothers were heroines in their neighborhoods and scouting was an after school "event."

Some of you may remember a grandparent who kept chickens or still used an "outhouse," being too proud to install one of those "new-fangled indoor toilets." But they taught us so many things: how to fish, how to hunt, how to sew, how to "make" a home. There were seasons too. There was marble season, top season, kite season, on and on. And as we grew, so did our ability to excel in sports or excel in studies. It was a simpler time, but it wasn't all that bad, was it? For as we all know, today the world is less safe, more complicated, full of bad dreams. But we can stop, if we give ourselves permission, and remember the good times… the good times.

It was a while ago that a longtime friend sent me a "snail mail" letter to share some of the things that were common to our lives as we entered our senior year in high school. I thought you might like to revisit some of them again, both in joy and in wonder. So here goes —

How hard is it to remember the days when girls in the gymnasium had really ugly uniforms? Or the days when nearly everyone's mom was home when we got back from school? How about the years during which male teachers wore neckties and female teachers had their hair done every day and wore high heels?

Wasn't it strange to drive into a gas station only to have your windshield cleaned, the gasoline pumped all for free, every time? And what an event it was to be taken out to eat by our parents and treated like a grownup! And do you remember the days when the teachers threatened to keep a kid back a grade if they failed… and then did it?

And it sure was fine to play baseball with no adults around. It was where we would "choose up" by tossing the bat back and forth to see who wound up with a hand on top to be the first to choose one's first team member.

When we went to the grocery store we found containers that would open easily because no one had tried to poison a perfect stranger. Those were the days when we dreaded getting home more than being sent to the principal's office for some prank. But there were no drive-by shootings, or drugs or "wilding" gangs.

Can you still remember names like Nancy Drew, the Hardy Boys, Laurel and Hardy, Howdy Doody and the Peanut Gallery – or the Lone Ranger, "The Shadow Knows," Roy and Dale, *I Love a Mystery*, or *Inner Sanctum*?

Perhaps sharing these remembrances occurred to me on our "Shared Seventieth High School Reunion" because I wanted to hearken to what indeed was probably "a better Era." Oh, and yes, remember the "double dog dare" and what it was?

Or, too, candy cigarettes, wax Coke-shaped bottles with colored sugar water inside. There were tableside jukeboxes in sandwich shops, Blackjack and Beemen's chewing gum and home milk delivery in glass bottles with cardboard stoppers.

Telephone numbers had a word prefix like Raymond 4-501. There were party lines, too. And peashooters, 45-RPM records, green stamps and Hi-Fi's. And can you recall Beanie and Cecil, roller skate keys, cork popguns, drive-ins and Studebakers?

How about visits by the Fuller Brush Man or Tinker Toys and Erector Sets? And Lincoln Logs. Baseball card packs were a nickel and contained a huge slab of bubblegum. Gasoline was thirty-five cents a gallon and cigarettes (which some of us smoked on the sly) were the same price, not $8.50 a pack.

And sometimes, with nothing else to do, we'd simply lie back on the grass with our friends; look up at the sky and say, "That cloud looks like..."

Ah, yes. The warmth of the good things remembered. A-a-a-men!

- J.V.K; Charlestown, Rhode Island '04

Father's Day - 2013

-contributed by Jana Knost Battiloro

My father taught me how to listen to music. By this I don't mean he only taught me about music, which he did. He spoke about Mozart with the same verve and excitement that some fathers speak about a football team or a favorite sport. By this I mean he literally taught me *how* to listen to a piece of music. I would sit, uncomfortably as an impatient nine or ten year-old, and I would squirm as I listened to Mozart's Piano Concerto in G Major, for instance, or Handel's "Hallelujah Chorus," or really any piece of classical or jazz music and I would watch my father sway slowly to the melody. He would, inevitably, at some point in the music, raise his finger in the air, close his eyes and lean back, as if the notes he heard were each separate, almost palpable, and he was literally tasting them as they entered his ears, just as if he were eating ambrosia. He would open his eyes at the end of a piece and look to my sister and me for a reaction (or maybe an agreement). "Isn't it wonderful?" he would ask, usually with his eyes brimming with tears. We would agree, but not with the same excitement I'm sure he was looking for. I would inevitably feel I had disappointed him because I did not understand (as most nine year-olds, save Mozart, do not) why a piece of music could make a person close his eyes, let alone cry. I was waiting for the big crescendo, the high note, the aria with the crashing cymbals to let me know that *this* was an important piece of music, *this* was worth waiting for.

What I did understand was that music was a piece of my father as much as his skin or his arms were. Music was what brought his parents together at the Eastman School of Music; music was what he enjoyed through the years as a child listening to the radio, before television was invented; music was what he explored through his learning of the drums and jazz music in the 1950s. Music was what he used as allusions in his sermons and punctuation in his church services. Music was what he used to express almost any emotion in our house, whether it was singing "Happy Birthday" or "Oh Danny Boy" – music was omnipresent in my father's life, and consequently our family's home.

What I did not understand, then, was that my father had been trying to show us that the notes, by themselves, are as beautiful as the melody's composition. That the sound of an instrument is as sacred as the song of a bird. That if you can throw back your head, close your eyes, and let a piece of music make you *feel*, then you are truly alive on the planet and you are a piece of the harmony itself. My father wasn't just teaching us to listen to music, he was teaching us to listen to our lives.

A couple of weeks ago I was home on a gorgeous Sunday morning. It was finally warm enough to have the windows open and I was puttering in my kitchen, cleaning up my family's breakfast and getting ready for the workweek ahead. I turned on Beethoven's Piano Sonata in C Minor and let it play, traveling in and out of the rooms of my house and my windows. I could see my neighbors across the street circling their garden, pointing and surveying the work they painstakingly put into the earth. I could hear the birds singing outside, along with the cicada who are visiting us for the next few weeks. My children laughed upstairs at each other as they played some version of house they had designed. I ignored the stressful week ahead of me and I listened to all of this music. I closed my eyes, threw my head back, and my eyes brimmed with tears at the beautiful music and the world around me. In that moment, I realized, I no longer wait for the crescendo in the music, I no longer wait for the big moments in life to feel, because my father taught me that you will miss the music entirely if you do. I listen to each note and marvel at the wonder of the world around us. My father taught me that.

Thank you, Dad. I love you.

SEXTONS, CUSTODIANS & JANITORS I HAVE KNOWN

One of my closest colleagues once said to a gathering of ministers, "How about each of us writing about the most unusual and interesting sexton our church employed?" The response was immediate and vocal. Such stories were legion. Unfortunately, that gathering of colleague experiences never got written. So, in keeping with my famous completion complex; let me offer just a few that I worked with over the years.

Walter. Walter was my mentor. I was a green "pulpiteer" serving in my first pastorate. He was a white-haired Roman Catholic who did his work and took a liking to me. Each day I would show up for office hours at nine. My office was in the sacristy just off the chancel of the sanctuary. At about ten, he'd lean his head into the staircase and say, very simply, "All hot, Reverend." That was a signal that he'd brewed us each a cup of tea. I would join him at one of the parish hall tables and we'd talk. Most of the time it was small talk. But once in a while he'd decide to give me some worldly advice about something I'd said. I remember one in particular. He said, "Reverend, you don't want to cross the women's group in your church, wherever it is. Believe me, I've eavesdropped their talk and they know what's going on. They can make you or break you, so try to stay on their side and help them out whenever you can." I never forgot his wisdom and I am grateful to him to this day for such guidance.

James. James always did his work, quietly, efficiently, on time without complaints. He was soft-spoken, friendly and quick to assist in whatever new program I was considering. For quite a while he would show up with a piece of men's jewelry as a gift. He brought cufflinks, tie clips, and a lapel pin or two. I never asked where he got them, although I suspect he worked for one of the local jewelry firms in that town.

Then there was Fred. Fred was a compulsive neurotic about his work. He was the only custodian I ever worked with who would show up in a three-piece suit to do his chores. He was well-groomed; perfectly coiffed and a stickler for perfection in the various tasks that were his to do in and around the church. One day I was standing with him just inside the door of the parish hall. The congregation was enjoying the usual after-service coffee hour – or what some Unitarian Universalists call "drinking the holy beverage." The ladies' alliance each week took pride in their hostessing. There were china cups and saucers, sterling silver flatware and sterling silver tea and coffee servers. Folks would line up, get their coffee, tea or juice and wander into groups around the room, enjoying the camaraderie and the lovely New England setting. But Fred was troubled. I said, "You look concerned, Fred. What's the matter?" He muttered something under his breath about all the snow and mud outside and then blurted out to me, "Look at what they're doing to my shiny, newly-waxed floor!" "Fred, that's what they pay you to do so that it looks good when they arrive." "I know, but it isn't fitting that they come stomping in here with their winter boots and make such a mess!" I never got over that moment.

Gerald. Gerald was a champion. He had several buildings under his care and the work got done – polishing floors, vacuuming, straightening up rooms, whatever. He was a family man who was proud of his kids. The church leadership knew what a fantastic worker they'd employed and they were always quick to provide him commensurate pay for his efforts. He had a smile that wouldn't quit and was a good friend. I was lucky.

Jim. Jim's regular work was as a driver for an MTA train on the Red Line in Boston. He was a time-stealer, asking me for a few minutes from time to time to agonize over his latest problem with various women. I'd just listen. What was I to do? He was an employee. But he didn't seem to notice that he never got much in the way of advice. Nevertheless, his plaintive stories continued. One of the legacies he left the church when he finally moved on was a basement full of paper products: paper towels, toilet tissue, paper napkins – you name it. He'd purchased it in huge cartons four feet on a side and the shipment filled two basement rooms in the parish hall. I suspect there was some sort of a "kickback" he enjoyed from the salesman who delivered it.

Dwayne. Dwayne was an enigma. Each morning at nine or so he'd look in on me in my office and say, "Good mornin', Mister Jan." Since Dwayne was African-American, I suspect this manner of salutation was taught him by his parents from birth. Then… he'd disappear. On that large church campus with five buildings, I'd never see him at work. Then, at about three each afternoon, he'd look in on me at my desk and say, "Well, Mister Jan, I'll be leavin' for home if it's alright with you." I'd say thank you and wave him on his way. But I never witnessed one stick of work he did. Some say he had a secret place on campus where he'd hole up and sleep the day away. How was old innocent me to know?

THE TERROR AND THE JOY

it sits and silence keeps;
a secret message undecoded
in its presence laying.
lazy seeming, as if asleep
with challenge that might be recorded;
a lofty aspiration beckoning.

joy might come
in fitful patches of light
within the dark,
but only if i pay the price.
insight, word and deed
could join the real world
held as if in ice.

contained within its being
(this shell, a-lingering, crouching there)
is terror all beyond imagining;
bright white, untouched;
potential in its ringing song.

stolid, still, suspenseful;
i pass it, guilty-filled.
(try not to notice)
(go right by)
(don't let the ghost be riled)
how many times a day
i pass this thing
and think upon the whitened terror

there within?
seldom do i bravely dare
approach its tempting
frightening blare
of sweet and sinister
substance that lies within.

i pass, re-pass
and tremble when i think what wonders
might become
if i, despite my sloth and circumstance of life
might more than touch
its hardened shell.

then,
reluctant hand outreached
to draw the terror
of a blank white page
to pen.

it is my desk
my study's desk
i love!
i hate!
i love!
(i guess)

REFLECTIONS IN A GLASS BOWL

L
ook you
at that gold
fish there in th
at small glass bowl.
Could it be that it is h
appy in its own world - even a
s small and hemmed in as
it is? I wonder? I
wonder that we
humans, like
that tiny

f

ish
find no anxious
preternatural force
urging itself
upon us
by the world
we live in .... or do we?
i

s
it a great and awe-inspiring
world
as we think it to be? ... yet forced by
our

81

efforts of haste and expediency
to diminish
day-by-day? Do we realize

h
ow little
we are …. and is it possible
that
some unseen force or reality observes us
as I view
this undersized carp?

ON WHAT MIGHT YET BE SAID

Yesterday's tomorrow… why
what a silly thing to say.
Why not say… "today?"
of course.

Why not say
what has been said
again?

We live our lives
in pigeonholes, sorting day by day
in units (60, 60, 24)
ad infinitum
…and someone takes the drastic step
and dares be true to what is seen.

The verdict? Condemnation!
The jury? Tradition! (but)
The reality? Truth (to be seen)
and riches for all!

And so; yesterday's tomorrow
is where we are right now;
a time that oft' claims no admirers since
they live either yesterday or tomorrow.

Oh! for a larger fraction of us all to live
all three… to see the greater whole
and find the wisdom in such a wondrous plan!

Jan Vickery Knost

You say a square has four sides?
I wonder when a square has five…?

Some brave soul someday will stand (and say it)
and so
when one does,
with kindness, take a second look
at what you first just say… with four!

Dedication to a Canine Friend

Doleful
tragic
loving
simple face that you could speak…

wretched
is the humble existence
that plagues you…

or so we think.

"Look, he's happy!"
"My, she's sad"… these words
betray opinion dull, insensitive, ignoble;
yet
our high-minded
    all-knowing
    omnipotent knowledge of all we think we see

finally places us in our humble niche of time.

For
to me
you're
a creature dear and yet, Dear God
but tell me
if
this one exists the same?
    apart from me?

Into brown eye I look, and wish I
could let life know what thoughts belie
or truly stand
I'd
speak a thousand thoughts at once;
and listen hard with myriad ear
to hear
all you have to tell.

Creatures, we
go the same way
as if in different veils of inconsistency.
Illuminated
only by a hope, a fear, a duty
as the genus or species we portray.

Ah!
But to love you
friend of man
with the tenderness
your eyes to me convey…

eternity would mark upon my soul
the love that I gave only in a dream.

- to Millard Fillmore, "the wonder dog"
of First Church, Dedham

VIRTUE

she sits against the sun-drenched wall
of church
appointed gaily in her gypsy scarf
and speaks with neighbors
of the day's events

their dialogue is short
                    horizon-limited
by each birth or death
  each day
  each meal
or church-confession heard

a mid-wife now
she serves the village
in ways quite un-like
to all that went before
for
now she brings new infant life
with gentle hands
into this simple world
where each resident
abides from off the land

but as she sits
remembering friends departed
eyes shaded from the now fast-falling sun
recalls
another time

when
she was to all
a source of warmth
not found in other arms

the distant village
where she'd lived
knew her as scarlet
woman – red
of puff and polish
   parlour soft
where each man would come
seeking
what they missed at home

her world, now offered up to God
                and church
is but the other side of joys she gave
wherein the church denied the pleasures
of the couch
thus to her came the men from out of homebed
chased except to procreate

how prostituted are the ones
who proudly show their reverence for God
for they become as hypocrites in their dumb
denying ways

                  - on sabbatical, Trebbiano, Italy, 1973

Yesterday's Tomorrow

- 1999

To bright red Inn they came
Bearing faith's universal name;
The Fraters, they
In constant ways
Brought us heritage of fame.

Today, remembered, all
Are enshrined in hearts made full;
We carry on
Their glorious song
In faith, hope and love, e'er long.

In years when we are gone
Our companions will come along;
To Wayside Inn,
Our home within,
We Fraters will reach beyond.

[Poet's note: may be sung to the tune of the hymn *"Send Down Thy Truth, O God"*]

"Fraters" are a group of Universalist ministers that have met every last weekend of January since 1902 for a religious retreat at Longfellow's Wayside Inn in Sudbury, Massachusetts. The author has been a member since 1964 and his Dad before him.

SLEEPING ANGELS

- Fall, 1974

Is night
the bed storm-toss'd
and mind is wandering
hammer-like
its beat
and goes from fear to fear
          work to play
the subjects toss'd
in sleepless billow
of the cover
over me
in bed.

Get up.

In nude and unpretentious body
go to larder
there to raid
and lose the troubled
wakefulness.

'Tis no success decreed.

Back up the stairs
of darkness – rooms
a-filled

with sleeping angels
wrought
from God's own gracious
giving hand.

I pause.

At the top of stairs turn left
and there she is
with thumb
and blanket
daughter – borne
amidst her dolls
security
she sleeps
as vision (kept in mind of God)
to re-create
her mother's lovely face
and form.

A-turning
cross the landing
steps but few
to room
that speaks potential
in a son of promise
and of joy.
First-born
his father's name he lives
in plan
that he will bring
in sons beyond his time.

Lonely.

Lonely, all this silence

wandering
in rooms
and mind
and night
'til finally
I come to her again
who is my help –
my love.

She moves
she moans in gentle dream-like
sleep
and gives her warmth
as easily to bed
as me she gives her love
             her trust
             her loyalty.

But when
with re-apportioned purpose
do I come to pillow
now no longer pounded
enemy…
but friend
I look across our room
at angel
still to come.

For there in
in corner
is an empty-aged cradle
lain in hope
some time in future
tense
we two
to fill.

The angel sleeps
in both our hearts;
not yet in cradle
only in the deep
and wondrous void
that future thus will tell.

My sleeping angels...
four.

BLUEBERRIES

- contributed by Peter Knost

Blueberries growing on John Varney's acres
Are highbush blueberries – nice easy takers.
No need to bend down while plucking a beauty;
The stiff Yankee back shuns unpleasant duty.

The Yankee has always found as his savior
Speech that's laconic and straitlaced behavior.
The highbush blueberries have long signified
The Yankee tradition to be dignified.

Now hard by the Varney's is old Prospect Mount
Where lowbush blueberries especially count.
The good Brothers Locke employ migrants to pick
From bushes whose berries are low and quite thick.

Such capable hands hail from sweet Carib isles,
Arriving with songs and sweet, generous smiles.
There's bending of backs and work isn't easy;
But listen awhile – their music is breezy!

New Hampshire trees such as maples and birches
Are reticent as the New Hampshire churches;
West Indian music beguiling the air
Cause taciturn forests to wonder and stare.

But since Yankee backs will not bend to the soil,
Un-Yankee pickers for berries must toil.
Of course, all in all it's a matter of taste,
For highbush or lowbush, they shan't go to waste.

DREAM ENCOUNTERED

-an odyssey of Laurel Brook

[N.B. This poem was written about a trout club whose members dream
of catching a fish from each of nine bodies of water* in one day between
sunrise and sunset.
    *Upper Brook, Basely, Pool, Peabody, Doctor's, Houghton,
    Joel, Mill Pond and Lower Brook]

The day was bright with sunshine and with promise
as he started into glis'ning dew-wet woods to Upper Brook.
Quite feverishly he arrow-bowed his rod
and flicked a gnat below a log and there he caught
his first.

Trout too small, released,
in gangly boots went flopping down the cartpath
'til ahead was Basely-view,
and there with different strategy he let a long and
lazy cast
proclaim pond surface, the first that day.
One rise of fish, another, then a third
until the thunder of a squaretail beaut was caught
and held
released.

Third at Pool was taken on an expert rollcast to
farthest shore
where from the moss and greenery shot a hungry

surge
of mouth and tail.
How well this long-planned venture goes, he mused
as on he hoofed to Peabody's
there to drift in lazy squarish craft, he
contemplated God.

The boat in which he sat, so still and floating free
carried him and hopes across without a strike.
"Oh, well," he thought, "I'll come again today to
Peabody."
And Doctor's to his mind sprang up – so –
clambering out, he shuttled off from Peabody's
to seek the fourth
within the waters of his favorite place.

The cast soared there
and rolled out to morning shadow 'cross the pool
then from the shadow into sun
a lightning bolt struck fast to claim proffered meal
- "That's four!"

"Back to Peabody's now to take a rainbow there?
Better still," he thought, "to Houghton's to try the
open spring."
He did, and that was five!

Then stopped by woods so still and not a city sound
to lunch with bird and lady slipper there,
a rich per cent of all the grandeur that was his that
day.

Then on to Joel's, to Mill Pond, fishing (fishing deep
for browns)
then Lower Brook, and, too, too quick
six, seven, eight! - - and nine?

The sun's shadows now grown long
this bright day dying
he backtracked fast to Peabody
but with a drift, another drift
his heart was sinking with the sun. "No triumph
here,
I've lost my victory for today."

Of all nine places no rainbow his at Peabody's.
"The daylight's gone and by agreement, I go, too."

The darkness then came sudden, sweet odyssey was
passed.
With dampened pride he came to lamplit
lodge
for rest, though unfulfilled.

The morrow yet an endless promise waiting,
and good time yet to capture hoped-for fish
in all those peaceful glades.

All Laurel Brook was his that day and almost
all the dream.
In Peabody, the rainbow, patient, wily,
waited.

- Dedicated to the memory of Walter D. ("Denny") Brooks; Member/
Treasurer of Laurel Brook Club from his friend and pastor, J.V.K. - 1973

THE PROMISE

nocturnal wand'rings
weeks-on-end
enslave the furried swain
to find his love

his mournful sounds of call
resound
thro' village streets
to make the list'ner wonder
at the perfidy
of nature

so sad it seems to human ear
come weal, come woe
his want is basic to his breed

he pads on pillowed feet to seek
the purpose god or nature thus has lain
upon his brain
eons ago

mournful though it sounds
the swain's nocturnal purpose
is, from love, enslaved

the cry, oft wailing in its theme,
is suddenly disturbed by new and simple dread,
competitor of older years is searching, too

the midnight darkness is disturbed
with crass and shrill
of violent claw
they growl, crescendo climbing
'til they clash
to rip each other's mask
of feline calm

then off, new victor,
there he goes
a-wandering, wandering
narrow paths
and ancient walls
archways, looming drafty, persons gone

so seldom is persistence
such as this rewarded
with its due
and when, with mate now-found
he lays in sensuous coup-ling ground
and sooths her tufted ear with new
less crisis-sounding verses of his whiskered mouth
does he remember
      remember wandering
            wandering in mournful
                  mournful cry
                       a-crying all those nights?

SOMEWHERE, ONE OF YOU...

the ruminations come in quiet dark
as supine sweating aging body creaks
to wakefulness
from sleep of shallow seldom kind
of church
of minister that is the body/mind and heart
of person called my own

arriving brain-born self-proclaimed
bearing me up to chancy time of worry
or of watchfulness
from out this chrysalis
of bed
again in answer to the call
to care

where? now? how?
when will it in ceasing stop this yearning
for peacefulness
announcing all is well
while knowing
it is not

for one of you   somewhere
it may not be!

O how to hold you all in my protecting
arms from hurt and woe of living
persevering wishing waiting

for a surcease to the pulse of life's
oft' bitter message of what's real

not truly possible a lot
but in my deepest heart
it's there that you abide
reside and safely rest
in joy and justice; life and love

be rest assured
it's known
you're there in absolute
and unremitting

care   (stay close!)

Livin' in the Red Dirt South

On the first day of school he and his brother were dropped off at the curb. Kids were already playing in the pine forest and schoolyard, yelling, shoving each other. The girls sat in little coveys staring at the boys. Occasionally, one would lean into the center and whisper something to her girlfriends and they'd all giggle.

The bell rang summoning all to their classes. The boy went down the hall to the sixth grade room the principal had indicated the day before on his visit there with his father. His brother went on to the fourth grade room.

As each classroom door closed, the building seemed to settle into a kind of slumber, the calls and slamming of doors echoing down its halls. An hour-and-a-half later those same doors would burst open and all the kids would stream back out into the play areas for recess. That was when it happened.

Being naturally shy, the boy had waited for his brother to emerge down the steps from his class. They sort of wandered around together, saying very little to each other or to their classmates. A trio of boys came over to them. Soon a couple more joined them. They circled the two, cutting them off from the sight of other kids playing.

The largest among them stood before the boy. He was barefoot and had freckles and a tousle of brown, unkempt hair. His feet were covered with the red dirt so typical of that part of the South.

"Hey, boy. What you mean playin' with that burrhead the other day?"

"I don't know what you mean," replied the boy.

"Yeah, ya do!" he said, giving the boy a push.

Another boy had crept in behind the boy and was down on all fours. The boy stumbled backwards and fell on the ground.

Suddenly, it was mayhem. Both the boy and his brother were on the ground with two or more boys on top of them, beating them in the face and stomach. Only the sound of the bell saved them from further onslaught. The attackers got quickly to their feet and ran for the school door. The two boys lay there, crying and wiping the blood from their faces. What had gone wrong? The day had started out with such excited anticipation of a new school, new friends.

It was not long before both boys realized that they had broken an unbreakable law. If that law had been written down it would have read: "In this town white kids will have nothing to do with black kids." The penalty for such an act was public humiliation and the beating they had just received.

Both boys dawdled as they walked to their father's car at day's end. They'd cleaned themselves up and were able to lie their way through the ride home. That night both of them had nothing to say to each other about that horrible experience. They just lay there in bed silently crying.

And that is how it all began. That is how a schoolyard beating changed the boy's life… forever.

*   *   *

The little grocery store stood on a slight rise in the road. In its parking lot you could see the sawmill and millponds filled with huge long leaf pine logs. Every so often the scream of a sawmill blade cut through the humid Alabama afternoon with a screech that was startling to visitors. But the town folks just went about their business.

The boy's "business" was a new job. At a proud thirteen years of age he'd gone to that grocery store and asked if there was any way he could work there. Now he stood before the manager, a tall, overweight man with black hair and bushy eyebrows. He looked at the boy and said, "Matter of fact there is. My carryout boy left town with his family two days ago. You can fill bags at the cash register and carry them out to the parking lot for our customers. Pays ten cents an hour… and when there's no one at the counter, you can stock the shelves. If you get a tip, you can keep it."

He remembered how he literally skipped home to tell his preacher father. Finally, a real job. How he'd dreamed of that moment! As he sat on the front porch of the parsonage he dreamed of all the things he could buy with all that money. He could go to the picture show anytime he wanted, even take his brother with him. And there was that miniature camera at the drugstore he wanted so much.

As he sat there looking out at the mansions owned by the mill owner families just up the street, he noticed a kid coming toward him on a bike. There was a baseball glove on the bike's handlebars. It hung there like the shield of a knight.

"Wanna' play ketch?" the boy shouted.

The kid skidded to a stop. "Yeah, sure."

Like a flash the boy went up on the porch and got his glove and ball.

Tossing the ball back and forth, the boy didn't notice the trio of kids walking up the street. They just watched, covertly. He didn't notice the scowls on their faces. Didn't notice that the kid who was throwing the ball to him had black skin. And certainly hadn't noticed the signs in all the public places that read, "Whites" and "Colored Here." For the boy had arrived only two weeks ago from California. His father had taken up his work with the new church people and had hardly been around home to tell him the difference.

At supper he proudly informed the family that he had a job after school. It was to begin the next day "To break him in" as his new boss had said.

"That's wonderful," said his mother from down at the end of the table.

His father didn't respond. He was absorbed in reading the daily newspaper.

"Did you hear our son, Richard? He's got a job!"

"Umph. Good boy, good boy," replied the man without looking up from his reading.

A little disappointed, but not surprised, the boy wolfed down his food.

The next day the boy was at the grocery store before the manager arrived. He sat on the pavement next to the front door of the store. Soon the manager's car swung into the parking lot and around to the side of the building.

"Morning, young man."

"Morning, sir." The boy spoke with a distinctly foreign manner.

The man looked at the boy. "Where you from, boy?"

"California, sir. My daddy's the new preacher up at the church on the hill."

"Oh, yeah. I heard that someone was comin' there to preach."

Without another word he pulled a great chain of keys from his pocket and fumbled among them to find the one that unlocked the store doors. "Come on. Time's a wastin'." As the boy followed him, he spoke into the darkened room. "There's two crates of canned peas you can get from the back. They go on the empty shelf in aisle two."

And so his day began. As he worked he began to notice that although the population of the little town where he'd come had a population of black and white people, none of the black people came to the store. Only white folks. It began to dawn upon the boy that there were rules. Rules unwritten, but rules nevertheless. To break these rules and "truck with those dark folk" was to be ostracized by one's peers.

On another occasion in that same schoolyard, feeling his power over the boy, the lead bully had criticized how the boy talked. "You talk funny, kid." With that he motioned to two of his friends. "Grab his arms!" Fearing a reprisal from their leader, the two boys caught him by the arms and held him. The large boy was lighting a cigarette. They were in the pine grove, out of sight of the supervising teacher. "I'll teach you to talk like us. Say, 'I hate niggers!' Say it!" Confused, the boy didn't know what he was talking about. "Say 'I hate niggers,' I said!"

With that, he puffed on the cigarette to make it red hot. He brought it down to the boy's wrist. Closer. Closer. "SAY IT, KID. SAY 'I HATE NIGGERS!'"

The boy only shook his head in denial, the tears streaming down his cheeks. Suddenly, as he heard the hiss of the cigarette meeting his flesh, he cried out in pain. Then there was no one. He dropped to the ground squeezing his wrist just above where the boy had burned him.

Though he had managed to keep his injury out of sight of the teacher, nothing of the kind was to happen when he got home. As it was weeks into the school year, he and his brother learned the way home and had walked together. He went straight to his room, not coming out 'til his mother called for supper.

Then it happened. His father arrived at the table. He noticed the boy's wrist as he sat down. He scowled. "What happened to your wrist, son?"

"Nothing, Dad."

"Yes it did. What happened?"

The boy sat for a moment, still. He knew he couldn't hold the tears any longer. He blurted out the story. Then he told about the beating he and his brother had received on the first day of school, too. It all rushed out, a flood of emotion spilling into the room as his bewildered parents sat there, speechless.

"He wanted me to say some word. Some word. It was... like... 'nigger'... yeah, that's it. The word he wanted me to say was 'nigger.' What's 'nigger,' Mom? What does it mean?"

Things were never the same in the parsonage after that meal. The lives of the two young boys were changed. They had been mentally raped by words and deeds so foreign to them that they were frightened every day. Survival became their watchword.

And that was how it was.

SIMPLICITY MADE DIFFICULT

The white, gleaming orb was in a state of grace – untouched, thus far, by the violent kiss of metal on its Surlyn cover. It was a golf ball – a Titleist ProV-1 – that required the highest rate of club head speed to launch it to its fullest potential.

The grass was a narrow highway of perfection, disappearing to the left around the stately trees that guarded its parameters. Above that was the "fair way," and the sky – a vision of blue with white flags of cloud.

He stood above the ball – square to the line of flight he intended for that white missile to take, and found his balance – a centering during which he rested – rested as a virtual tripod of leg-leg-shaft and clubface – just before his mind's initial call for energy.

Breathe. Long breath. Release. And calmness – the closing of the eyes to visualize the path – glancing left to see "The Way," then calm, again.

With deep-intentioned catch of breath, the swing – the swing away – began. Low and slow – the arms stiff, hands with firm pressure – squeeze right – until all the way back, the left shoulder felt slight pain of full extension. Then, the slow shifting of his weight and downward descent of hand, the club head now a blur of brightness just before the "p-i-in-n-g-g!" which rang the bell of ignition and takeoff!

His eyes, thro' all of this, had never left that milk-white sphere. He saw it even through the millisecond of impact – then drove through with his hands to finish high and away – and only then did he look up.

It flew – that ball – a course of true perfection – low to high and rising to an apogee – it hung there for an infinitude of time, then turned a bit to land, near out of sight around the corner of The Way – and very near the place that's called "The Green."

This one and only brief moment of perfection was, he felt, a time at which he stood at heaven's gate.

A Story with No Name

-contributed by Lorna Smith Knost

It is December 21st. It is the anniversary of the death of someone I never knew and yet, we all know him only too well.

A group of us from church had chartered a bus to travel the thirty or so miles to New York City. We were attending a celebration of the winter solstice. It was to be an evening of music in the beautiful Cathedral of Saint John the Divine with the Paul Winter Jazz Consort. On this, the shortest day of the year, we would raise our voices in harmony and our hopes with music to push back the darkness and welcome the light.

We gathered to travel on a Greyhound bus. There we were, the demographically predictable group of Unitarian Universalists – former Methodists, Congregationalists, Presbyterians, Catholics, Jews and previously un-churched; educated, affluent and upwardly-mobile. With our disposable cups of white wine, wedges of brie and a hired designated driver, we began our journey.

As the bus rolled on, we began to sing Christmas carols; encouraged, I am sure, by the outdoor lights, falling snow and a general sense of well-being and euphoria with the season which was, no doubt, heightened by the contents of our Styrofoam "chalices."

The "Noels" soon segued to gospel hymns. We stony Unitarian Universalists who remembered *all* the verses to "The Old Rugged Cross," "Shall We Gather at the River?" and "Bringing in the Sheaves" sang with joy and gusto. "How about this one?" someone would say, and we'd all join in.

And then the bus slowed and finally stopped. We were in the city. I cannot remember what street we were on then, but it doesn't really matter. Not a whole lot in the city seemed to matter, I thought, and we sang on.

My attention turned and I looked out my window. There, lying lifeless at the front wheels of a bread truck, was the body of a street person. His few possessions and brown paper bag "suitcase" scattered in the slush. Someone's son... or father... or brother? Did anybody know him, I thought. Who will care? Where *is* everyone? All I can see are two policemen and the city ambulance crew. Others walk on by.

How unceremonious it all is, I thought. This isn't right! It's Christmas. He belongs to someone. But no, there will be no glowing obituaries in *The New York Times*.

I realized then that I was still singing softly, as were my friends. And indeed, from the most unlikely source of all – this group of Unitarian Universalists who long ago had stopped singing the "amen's" to close hymns and fairly warbled through *Hymns for the Celebration of Life* – were singing the old gospel hymn, "Amazing Grace," with emotion and caring.

It seemed to me that at that moment, we were truly "the priesthood of all believers" as we offered our last rites. And so, for that man on the street; that crumpled, dead figure who surely knew love once, however ephemeral, and who was no less a child of the earth, we bestowed our "blessing."

Each winter solstice I think of that episode. I sing a verse of "Amazing Grace," play a Paul Winter album, wish I *could* make things all right with the world – but, at my best, strive for the few stumbling, good turns that I *can* do. Then, I quietly and humbly offer my remembrances and another blessing for John Doe.

(First written and shared with the congregation of the First Unitarian Church in Summit, New Jersey – Christmas, 1984.)

THE KISS

Tom sat at the edge of the bed trying to wake up after his afternoon nap. He enjoyed them more frequently now and he looked forward to them. He sat there looking at his hands. She'd always admired his hands. She said they made her feel loved. Now they were gnarled, liver-spotted. He clenched them a couple of times, releasing the stabs of arthritic pain. "Forgot the ibuprofen," he thought to himself as he gathered his forces to rise from his bed and go and do a very important part of his daily life.

She sat there in the hall with the daily phalanx of wheel-chaired residents. Each afternoon they were rolled there, lined up like cordwood against the wall. They waited, seemingly forgotten. She sighed.

They had come to the residence a year ago, made friends, had little tiffs with each other and with neighbors. But it was good at first. But now, through the cruelty of house policy and the neutrality of life's process, they were separated. She lived in a dorm where someone could "look after her." He had a room alone, two halls away.

Tom thought of their lives together as he combed his hair. He didn't know why but he had not lost that battle others had waged. His hair was as thick as a teenager's, only now it was snowy white. He remembered their college days; their courtship, their wedding. They had worked together, had children, faced bills and family problems. Through it all they had raised their three sons who all lived away. Their visits were infrequent at best. But both Tom and his beloved counted themselves fortunate. He sighed.

Now the days seemed so meaninglessly long, so empty. He missed her daily presence so much; her gentle, quiet assurance, her warmth of spirit. But he knew. It was for the best. That's what they said. And so he had struggled, as had she, with the finality of their new lives apart.

Turning carefully to reach for his cane lest he stumble again and risk a broken hip like his neighbor, he tottered to his dresser. There were the meager artifacts of a long life. His pocket watch still ticked and chimed the hour to the delight of any admirer. His lapel pins shone on the counter – lodges, clubs, honorary societies. The pictures were of their sons, their grandchildren, their farm. He sighed again, thinking, "so much water under the bridge." Happily, and his heart beat a bit faster, was her visage captured in an oval frame.

The face that looked out from that frame was beautiful. She had had long, dark tresses. Her cheekbones were high, giving her face the appearance of nobility. Her nose was aquiline, her mouth full. The strength was in her eyes. Her portrait evoked a sense in the viewer of wanting to have known this person. She seemed so sure of herself. She seemed kind. And a subtle smile suggested a warm sense of humor.

What wonderful years, what fine experiences they'd enjoyed. When adversity came, they were a team; partners. When wronged, they had contested and usually emerged the better for their struggles. It had been a marriage of love, of work and of luck. Only once had there been doubts.

It was while Tom was away on a long assignment. The miles were too many to allow the luxury of a return. She had wondered at his fidelity since one of his working partners had been a woman of singular means and attractiveness. When she questioned him on his return, her answer was in the tears that welled in his eyes. She knew.

Filled again with the need to be with her, Tom started toward the door, tapping the cane ahead of him. Frail now in his nineties and wishing his old legs would move a little faster, he continued on. But patience ensued and though mumbling a quiet curse or two to himself about his pace, he opened the door and turned into the hall.

There, all was movement and electric activity. The white-garbed residence assistants were all about. "There's our dear one!" said one. "Good morning, Tom," said another. A third patted him on the shoulder as he passed. "He's a darlin', that's for sure."

It was a little sad, he thought to himself. "Don't they realize that the 'good resident' is the one who doesn't ask for anything? Oh, well… whatever." He continued down the hall. And so they sat, waiting for someone to move them to the next event of the day – breakfast, beauty parlor, lunch, naptime, music, chapel, dinner, bed. So it went. Once in a while there was the inevitable empty bed, its resident departed. Sometimes the news was that a relative had moved them home or to a less-expensive home. Sometimes they died.

There, past the nurses' station were the wheelchairs. A daunting sight. Some sagged with their heads back, staring into space. Others were curled into a seemingly hopeless paralysis, giving the appearance of death, which, for many, wasn't far off. A couple were bright and cheery, looking about, animated. Tom passed them, greeting as many as would greet him back. At the end of the line he reached his destination.

Slumped in her chair was his beloved. She seemed asleep. Her body gave the appearance of infinite exhaustion. Her hair was straggly, in snarls. The attendants hadn't gotten around to combing what thinning locks she still retained. Her skin was clear, but lined with many years and the cares only a mother could know. So she sat, waiting, waiting.

Tom's step increased. His tap-tapping cane's crescendo rose as it danced its way toward her. And then he stopped. He was just to the side of her chair. Bending laboriously so that his lips were close to her ear, he whispered gently to her, "How's the prettiest girl I've ever known? How's my bride today? I'm so glad to see you, sweetheart."

Slowly, almost imperceptibly, she raised her head. Her eyes shone in gratitude that someone she loved was there. Through rheumy eyes, she focused on her man. How she loved him. And here he was, just as handsome as ever.

A tear glistened as she replied, "Oh, Tom, you tell a lie so well. But I surely love it, I really do. Here…"

She raised her face to him. He leaned his cane against her chair and steadied himself on the chair's arm. With his other hand, he cupped her precious, aged face. He leaned down, slowly, carefully, until, with just the slightest touch, their lips met.

"I love you, Tom."

"I love you, too. May I take you to dinner?"

She held his cane as he wheeled her into the dining room.

BIBBLE, BABBLE, BIBLE –
WHAT TO TEACH?

Once upon a time a church member asked me what I would teach Unitarian Universalists in a course about the Bible. I thought it an intriguing question and did consider it seriously for some time before giving up on the possibility. I suspected it would be very difficult to keep the attention of an adult class for the time it would take to do it well. On the other hand, were I to design a proposal for a course on Scripture for today's Unitarian Universalist theological students, it would be an entirely different matter, indeed.

At the outset I would like to tender a gentle warning on what's to come. I promise you, it will not be the usual "yada-yada-yada" that always seems to happen when people get dewy-eyed in speaking about "The Holy Book."

At Saint Lawrence University, my Bible professor was Doctor Morton Scott Enslin. I came to love him, respect him and fear his exams. I can still recall his ruggedness. As regular as clockwork he would arise at five a.m. and take a cold bath, smoking his pipe as he studied his notes for his classes. And yet, notwithstanding his tough exterior, he would frequently give vent to tears when referring to Scripture. "You've got to love it. Prize it. Possess it with all your being." This resulted in a quiet respect for the subject he was teaching in most of his students. But that's not the kind of sentimental claptrap Bible pundits of today resort to in order to trap their hearers. His was a genuine love of the subject.

On the other hand, Doctor Enslin did not journey into the more troubling portions of Scripture, being content to point our attention to the main currents of literature, history and the prophets it contains. I suspect he chose not to instruct us in some of the more troubling aspects of the Bible relying upon us to find it out for ourselves. That the Bible does contain real paradoxes in its makeup is a well-known truth. That point has been made over and over again down through history by conservative and liberal thinkers. It was James Cardinal Gibbons who wrote that:

"A competent religious guide must be clear and intelligible to all, so that every one may fully understand the true meaning of the instructions it contains. Is the Bible a book intelligible to all? Far from it; it is full of obscurities and difficulties not only for the illiterate, but even for the learned."

- James Cardinal Gibbons; *The Faith of our Fathers, VIII,* 1876

A major portion of my proposal, then, will deal with some of these difficulties. I would not do so, however, without taking pains to assist my class in the very basics of the Bible and its history. During the first weeks of the first semester of a course on the Bible, I would give my hearers a very general outline. Obviously, the parameters of such an investigation would be huge. But it is mandatory that students be acquainted with the basic facts and figures of any topic before delving into the more complicated issues and concepts about it. Having done that, ascertaining by discussion and exams that my students had a working knowledge of what the Bible is *and* where to go to investigate it further, I would proceed on a new tack.

Perhaps I would begin the first lecture for this next section of my course with a quotation from *The Age of Reason* by Tom Paine (1794). Here was his caveat regarding how one should approach the Bible. He wrote:

"Whenever we read the obscene stories, the voluptuous debaucheries, the cruel and torturous executions, the unrelenting vindictiveness, with which more than half the Bible is filled, it would be more consistent that we called it the word of a demon than the word of God. It is a history of wickedness that has served to corrupt and brutalize mankind."

- Tom Paine; *The Age of Reason,* 1794

Just for a moment, imagine yourself suddenly the victim of a Biblically-based attack. Unitarian Universalist kids in the Bible Belt have this happen to them all the time, usually in the schoolyard. And we know that in our crypto-conservative religious world today, Scripture, whether Judaic, Muslim or Christian; is often used as a means to control, to vilify, to limit behavior or to make people afraid. It is also used more and more, unfortunately, to shape public opinion (if the current Bush administration is any indication of the same).

A prime example of this during the origins of the Jewish people was the "Holiness Code" that was drawn out as a way of conduct for the Levites. It had several themes which, when put in the vernacular, might read: "Eat the flesh of the swine and die." "Practice masturbation and die." "Enter into adultery and die." "Become pregnant outside of wedlock and be stoned to death."

There were other ways in which Scripture shaped human behavior and human opinion. The Holy Scriptures have been used to justify slavery *and* to justify the abolition of slavery. They have been used to justify the superiority of white Protestants and to prove an Afro-American presence in the Bible.

It has justified civil rights as well as reasons for persecuting the Jews. It has been employed to define the traditional role of women, to provide sanctuary for political refugees and to empower and liberate the poor. The accusation and execution of women as witches can be found in its pages. In today's world, it has been used to oppose the ordination of women and the ordination of gay priests.

My *King James Bible* contains nearly 1200 pages that include the Old and New Testaments. In them I can find its definition of human behavior for many things as well as the punishments for doing wrong. Sodomy, abortion, the physical punishment of children, for the wearing of certain clothing and hairstyles, all these and more. The book is replete with a commentary on all manner of life.

In it one can find the good and the bad, the liberal and the conservative elements going hand in hand. For instance, you can find reasons for the causes of certain diseases. Former Attorney General John Ashcroft could find passages to justify discrimination, intolerance and violence toward homosexuals and others he deemed "unclean." What to do, then? How to teach? What illustrations would one use to capture the mind of the reluctant student?

Well, Ralph Waldo Emerson had a suggestion. He once said the following:

"Make your own Bible. Select and collect all the words and sentences that in your reading have been like the blast of triumph out of Shakespeare, Seneca, Moses, John and Paul."

Thomas Jefferson had already acceded to this plan by producing his little volume titled simply, *The Jefferson Bible*. Countless other authors have tried to modernize Scripture to their own ends, good and/or bad. So it goes.

As some of you know, I grew up in the deep South. Richard Knost left a perfectly respectable and successful ministry in San Jose, California, where he had built a church from a membership of zero to over 250 in three short years. Suddenly, I learned that we would be moving to a place called Brewton, Alabama. "Brewton, Alabama, Dad?? Where's that?"

In later years I came to realize that those six years of my growing up became central not only to my religious "becoming" but to my thinking regarding the Holy Scriptures of the Old and New Testaments. I say this for a number of reasons.

First and foremost, school began each and every day with a reading from Scripture chosen by the teacher and read by a student, and a recitation of the Pledge of Allegiance to the Flag of the United States of America – *without*, I might add, the phrase, "…under God" as a part of that pledge.

Outside the classroom, most students were steeped in the Biblical tradition. Classmates spoke of learning the Bible in Sunday School and of taking part in what they called "Sword Drills." Each student would stand at attention, Bible under the arm. The teacher would speak out this or that chapter and verse of this or that Book, Old Testament or New. The first student to find it jumped forward out of line and was invited to read it. If correct, points were awarded for success and long chains of award bands were worn proudly to school.

What was our favorite song – a song unquestioned by anyone? It was composed of words written by Susan Warner in 1860 in a book entitles, *The Love of Jesus* and it went:

> *"Jesus loves me, this I know,*
> *For the Bible tells me so."*

- Susan Warner; The Love of Jesus, 1860

This kind of culture did not seem to impact too badly upon my brother or me. In fact, one of our best friends was the son of the local Baptist pastor and we never discussed religion. One day we were out riding our bikes on a Saturday morning. Our clothes were always the same: blue jeans, white tee shirts, barefoot, and with a baseball glove on the handlebars of our bikes.

As we pedaled down the dirt alley between the Baptist Church and some residences, my brother skidded his bike to a stop. "What's that?" he asked our friend.

"Oh, that's the cistern that collects rainwater for the baptismal font in the church."

My brother leaned his bike against the wall of the cistern then jumped up, one foot balancing him on the seat of the bike and peered over the side. "Hey, it's deep! I'm going swimming."

In no time he had his tee shirt and blue jeans off. (We always had our bathing suits on under our jeans since we regularly went to "O'Bannion's Wash Hole" to swim on the weekends.)

"I don't think that's a very good idea," said our Baptist friend.

But when I followed, so did he. We were splashing around in the cistern when I came up and said, "What's that big pipe down there? Where does it go?"

"It goes to the baptismal font, but I don't think…" All he could see were two pairs of feet diving down. So he followed.

When we came up into the sanctuary baptismal font and surfaced for air, there was the Ladies Bible Study Group holding their weekly Saturday morning chapel! Self-evidently, we didn't see our Baptist friend for weeks and got a pretty serious dressing-down from our dad as well.

While living in Houston, my wife, Lorna, was employed as the Director of Religious Education for the First Congregational Church of Houston. The minister's wife there was one Maggi Tucker, a musicologist of the first order; organist, choral director, composer and editor of the newest Congregational hymnal, *Hymns of Truth and Light*, a volume of nearly 600 pages becoming more and more popular with mainstream UCC churches. Maggi told me a story one time about the ethos of the hymn, *Onward, Christian Soldiers*. It helps to shed light on the problems that come with the various translations of the Bible.

She said it had been composed as a marching song for a British boys' school to be used as they went singing from village to village or when they processed up and down the school chapel's main aisle. One day, the boy who was supposed to carry the cross forgot it. He left it where it was stored behind a sacristy door. When the boys left the chapel and discovered the oversight they ended up singing, "Onward, Christian soldiers, marching as to war, with the cross of Jesus left behind the door!" There are many examples where the difficulty of words or the changing of words had a reason based upon historical happenings. I suspect this apocryphal story is not one of them. So...

Enough of levity! Let me return to my proposal. My students would have to become aware of the many translations and versions of the Bible the world contains. Listen to some, but not all, of the translations of Holy Scripture that have come down to us through history:

The William Tyndale Bible
Miles Coverdale Bible
Thomas Matthews Bible
Geneva Bible
Douai Reims Bible
King James Bible
The Moffat Translation
The Goodspeed Translation
The English Revised Bible
The American Standard Bible
The Revised Standard Bible
The New English Bible

Jewish Versions
Catholic Versions
The Blue Letter Bible.

There are also later Modern Versions according to the Dutch, French, Germans, Hungarians, Italians, Portuguese, Scandinavian, Slavic, Spanish and Swiss. And probably hundreds more. Everyone over the years seems to have felt that there was a better way to translate it or tell it.

> "Oh, that pestilent book! Never on it more
> look –
> I wish I could sing it out louder –
> It has done men more harm, I dare boldly af-
> firm,
> Than th' invention of guns and of powder."
> - Anonymous; *The Catholick Ballad,* c. 1550

Or, to put it in John Greenleaf Whittier's words:
> "Foul shame and scorn be on ye all
> Who turn the good to evil,
> And steal the Bible from the Lord
> And give it to the devil."
>
> - John Greenleaf Whittier; *A Sabbath Scene,* 1850

Beyond all these paeans of praise and cries of derision regarding Holy Scripture though, I need to be a little more realistic. The Bible *is* fraught with difficulties. It is *not* the "revelations of God" as asserted by the orthodox, but a product of human effort. Read it on a daily basis and I promise you (as I would my students) a veritable rollercoaster ride. For the Bible takes one up and down, threading inconsistencies with hard line commentaries on the human condition. It contains some of the most beautiful poetry in the world as well as merciless records of human cruelty, greed, corruption, lust and all the failures common to humanity.

Let me continue with a few pointed comments regarding the difficulties I alluded to at the beginning of this paper. As references I would mention but three. One is titled *The X-Rated Book: Sex and Obscenity in the Bible* by J. Ashleigh Burke (The American Bible Society – 1976). The other is called *An Underground Education: the unauthorized and outrageous supplement to everything you thought you knew about art, sex, business, crime, science, medicine (religion) and other fields of human knowledge* by Richard Zacks (Doubleday – 1997). And finally, a wonderful little volume by Miles R. Abelard (apparently an acquaintance of my father) titled *Physicians of No Value* (Reality Publications – 1983). I was not able to resist including Mister Abelard's unique, old world subtitle. It reads:

Physicians of No Value –
being
a Terse, True and Entertaining
Compendium
of
religious sense and nonsense
documenting selected
Biblical CONTRADICTIONS and absurdities
together with other
ecclesiastical flummery of science, history and moral
along with
Neglected and Pertinent Religious History
for the enlightenment of
PROSELYTIZERS and other ECCENTRICS
who may wish or need to
RATIONALLY EVALUATE
certain
religious travesties, sophistries and tribal mores
deriving from the
DARK AGES
together with various
SUGGESTIONS
for the
repair and rebuilding

of an
Amoral Society
victimized by
Iatrogenic Spiritual Ailments
caused by pious Quack Doctors of the Soul
"Forgers of lies" and "Physicians of no value."

(Job 13:4)

In his chapter titled "Bible Contradictions and Paradoxes," Mister Abelard writes:

"So there have been editors and interpolations – some subtle, some blatant. This is God's work? You've got to be kidding. This is your God, who makes copying errors, who contradicts himself repeatedly? This, the textbook on which you evangelists lavish so much loving, scholarly attention – the one and only, be-all and end-all source you search and research for devious clues to the meaning of existence? As well to search Mother Goose hoping to find Boyle's Law or Avogadro's number! …how in the name of all that is sane can you proselytizers and evangelists so arrogantly force on others what you so naively term the 'truth' all the while blindly ignoring …newer, thoughtful, god-given modern sources of revelation as if they had no existence?" (Pgs. 9-10)

Burke and Zack give us insights into the more indecent (shall I say "conveniently forgotten"?) portions of the Bible. Here are some a prudent professor might wish to impart to his or her students by means of a reading list. A discussion in class would probably become the talk of the campus!

Says Zack:

"Racier than any daytime talk show, the Bible packs incest, castration, beheadings, cross-dressing, polygamy, sex slaves, seduction, baby murder, and that's just the first few hundred pages. Smack in the middle of Deuteronomy (25:11-12) we learn that a wife who helps her husband in a fight by grabbing his enemy's testicles shall have her right hand cut off. In the Book of Samuel II (16-20) we find the son of King David insulting his Dad by having sex with ten of his father's concubines on a rooftop for all of Israel to see."

125

King Saul was suspicious of David and feared him, too. David wanted to marry Saul's daughter but Saul was opposed to it. So Saul instructed his officials to tell David that "all the King wants from you as payment for the bride are the foreskins of a hundred dead Philistines, as revenge on his enemies." (Actually, Saul hoped David would be killed by the Philistines.) David was delighted with the thought of becoming the King's son-in-law and went out and killed *two hundred* Philistines. According to the Biblical account, David took the foreskins before the King and counted them all out before him, one-by-one.

We learn from Burke that when Moses laid down the Ten Commandments he also laid down rules of engagement for battle that would break every mandate of the Geneva Convention. He instructed his troops to kill and rape all the women and keep all the girls who are virgins. (Numbers 31:13-18)

So one would find that virgins figure largely in Scripture. But the killing of male children and the capturing of children and women was pretty typical for Biblical warfare as well as premiums placed on proving that a new bride was a virgin.

One of the strangest punishments meted out by the Lord God was the command to the children of Israel to eat human excrement (Ezekiel 4:12-13):

"And thou salt eat it as barley cakes, and thou shalt bake it with dung that cometh out of a man, in their sight. And the Lord said: Even thus shall the children of Israel eat their defiled bread among the Gentiles, whither I will drive them."

On the more humorous side there were miscellaneous Laws laid down. One was a rule for soldiers in a camp (Deuteronomy 23:12-14):

"You are to have a place outside the camp where you can go when you need to relieve yourselves. Carry a stick as part of your equipment, so that when you have a bowel movement you can dig a hole and cover it up." (One would opine that even God, in his walks through a camp to bless his people, didn't want to step in it!)

It was okay to own slaves and even to beat them. But if one did so and the slave died the instigator was to be punished. However, if, after a day or two, the slave lives, the master was not to be punished since the loss of his property was punishment enough.

Polygamy was widely practiced, as we all know, and there were rules for polygamy that could probably be found, as well, in the Koran. Here are two:

"If a man takes a second wife, he must continue to give his first wife the same amount of food and clothing and the same rights that she had before." (Ex. 21: 10)

and:

"No man is to disgrace his father by having intercourse with any of his father's wives."

I can only say in conclusion (applause here!) and after having researched a little more deeply than was required in theological school, that it would be a singularly difficult task to teach a course on Holy Scripture with any kind of completeness. The topics are so far-ranging, so complicated, so open to interpretation that it would turn out to be a lifelong task and the sure knowledge of falling short after all. Suffice it to say that perhaps Doctor Enslin's passionate praise of the Bible as beautiful literature that one must embrace and love, notwithstanding its contradictions and paradoxes, would be the best one could expect to do as a teacher of the same.

The prime reason I say this is because one never knows what one is going to find in the Bible. Even the wisest *Midrash** many times falls short. But I hope the references I have made in this very inadequate attempt to tackle the assignment will be accepted in the spirit of Robert Frost's little couplet:

"Forgive, O Lord, my little jokes on Thee,
And I'll forgive Thy great big one on me."

Finis

*In Judaism, the collected rabbinical commentaries and explanatory notes on the Scriptures, written between the beginning of the Exile and c. A.D. 1200.

THE SUNSHINE OF THE SOUL

"Laughter is the most successful weapon against
the depravity of the human race."

- Mark Twain

There is no secret about the fact that this congregation has faced its challenges over the past. In times like these, no matter the situation, there are ways to re-establish spiritual wholeness. My hope is that during the next few minutes we might discover one of those ways.

Once in a while someone says to me, "C'mon, Jan. Lighten up!" Most of the time, I know exactly what's implied. I'm either going to fast or taking things too seriously. Sometimes it's because I'm not taking care of my own mental and spiritual health. And I suspect that this charge might be true of most of us from time to time. Our dedication to "the task" sort of gets out of hand. And this can become true of congregations as well.

This morning's message, then, is dedicated to what has been called "R and R." My hope is that it will become an opportunity for us to take some time in which to rest and refresh ourselves. There is no doubt that the human condition requires such leisure, both intellectually and spiritually. We need to give our inner selves a chance to breathe and not take ourselves so seriously.

Permit me to say what I consider a "truism." Laughter, joy or humor and religion should appear on the same page from time to time. In pursuing this quest I would share a brief quotation made by the American humorist, James Thurber. He wrote:

"If a thing cannot endure laughter, it is not a good thing. Laughter is never out of date or out of place. Too often the intense person loses their ability to laugh and accuse those who see humor in pompous circumstances of being sacrilegious. Far from it! Parody, satire and wit represent strong emotions, for we usually parody and satirize only those things which mean

128

something to us, and when we use those forms with love and affection, we are paying homage. Thomas Carlyle said, 'True humor springs not more from the head than from the heart; it is not contempt, its essence is love.'"

Most Unitarian Universalists possess a good sense of humor, notwithstanding those zealots who seem invariably to have their most important cause or causes. And it's okay to laugh at ourselves. In fact, there are a lot of stories *about* Unitarian Universalists. We just get a little perturbed when someone from another faith tells a joke at our expense since it's usually told in contempt. It would be difficult, for instance, for a member of the inner circle of government of the Mormon Church to understand why we would laugh at the following scenario.

We Unitarian Universalists have long been the object of jest over the topic of prayer. The question might be phrased something like this: "If the God you worship is described by you as First Cause, Natural Effect, Causal Order, and not a personal god, who can answer your prayers? What is the object of your supplications? Upon being asked this question, we are told that one Unitarian Universalist responded, "We just pray 'to whom it may concern.'"

We also have problems with communication. We love to use words like "process." There are those who cherish being able to "interface" with each other. Some might say they "resonate" to what their sisters and brothers say to them. And, oh, yes, we have sensitivity marathons, workshops that run for months, parent effectiveness training courses and we talk, talk, talk. But sometimes, in all that esoteric talk, one essence of life called humor… may be missing.

Why emphasize humor in one's life? What function does it serve? Psychologists define it academically in a way that is almost comical:

"Laughter is a reflex characterized by the coordinated contraction of fifteen facial muscles in a stereotypical pattern, with the drawing back and slight uplifting of the corners of the mouth, the raising of the upper lip, and the curving of the furrows between mouth and nostrils. It is accompanied by altered breathing, an interior convulsion, and increased brightness of the eyes."

Well… my comment in response to that way of explaining humor is, "That may be accurate, but it sure doesn't get at the gist of what happens when humor occurs!"

I will agree that humor is *not* a simple reflex. For instance, when light is shown into the eye, there is a contraction. When a pin is stuck in the skin, there is a reactive jump caused from the pain. Stimulus – Response. But it is really difficult to understand the complicated mental activity which occurs when one reads familiar cartoons such as *Classic Peanuts*, *The Wizard of Id*, *Dilbert*, or, you name your favorite. The responses that result from different people encountering something "funny" have puzzled philosophers for centuries. Why do people laugh?

According to Aristotle, laughter was closely related to ugliness or debasement. For Cicero, it was connected to fear, cruelty or deformity. For Descartes, it was a manifestation of joy mixed with surprise and, of all things, hate. In a more modern idiom, theologian/philosopher Henri Bergson asserted that laughter was a veiled threat to humiliate and correct a neighbor. According to the *Oxford Dictionary*, humor originally referred to moisture or juice.

Moving along in our "all-star review" we learn that since the 17th century, humor has come to mean the quality of action, speech or writing that excites amusement. It also refers to the human faculty of perceiving what is ludicrous or amusing. Humor, represented as moisture, can truly *have* a symbiotic lubricating effect on one's life, giving our lives new freshness and flavor.

Taking our investigation to another tack, humor can also be a passive-aggressive defense that sometimes preys on human tragedy. When this happens, we experience a sense of malice, derision or condescension. Overall, however, humor and the laughter it brings is a way of finding balance. It is a worthy security against the trap of self-pride and conceit. And, it is the strongest inducement for finding patience and resilience in the face of human suffering.

I have a retired colleague named David Rankin. For many years he was minister of the huge Fountain Street Church in Grand Rapids, Michigan. In our evening sessions after ministers' conferences, he liked to tell a story of what happened during his ministry in the First Unitarian Church of San Francisco. He was asked to perform a wedding for a couple. Believe it or not, the groom was the famous comedian, Red Skelton. While waiting for the service to begin, this inimitable humorist looked down at the courtyard that contained the grave of a former minister. He turned to David and said, "Gee, they sure do treat you guys rough around here!"

One of the more familiar figures in human history that has always typified our topic is the clown or jester. These were the wits who softened truth for the monarch, many times at the risk of their own necks. They used pathos, slapstick, pratfalls and imitations of infirmity. These were comic devices based upon weakness and human limitation. Parody and other forms of humor rely upon a kind of degradation for their success. I once played the part of Jack Point in the Gilbert and Sullivan light opera *Yeoman of the Guard*. Jack Point is the main character. He is the jester. He is also in love with his ward, Elsie Maynard. But it cannot be. And so he suffers from afar, having been outwitted in his pursuit of love. He sings (and forgive me):

"When a jester is outwitted,
Feelings fester, Heart is lead.
Food for fishes, Only fitted.
Jester wishes he was dead.

O the doing and undoing,
Oh, the sighing and the suing,
When a jester goes a-wooing
and he wishes he was dead.
He wishes… he… was dead."

I have a slightly different theory regarding the question of why there is humor and how laughter happens. I grew up on a small southern Alabama town called Brewton. My Dad was minister of the Universalist Church there. During those years, my brother and I spent our Saturday mornings at the Ritz movie theater. Going to the movies in those days was a blessed event for kids. Each week we'd see a couple of short westerns, a couple of serials, three or four cartoons and the *Movietone News of the World*.

Sometimes there would be a movie such as *Abbott and Costello Meet the Wolfman*. Or there'd be one of several films made by the Bowery Boys. There was also a liberal sprinkling of the Three Stooges and an occasional visit from Laurel and Hardy.

It was a time of popcorn, soda and laughing uncontrollably in the darkness and learning *how* to laugh. Sometimes we tend to overlook the fact that, for kids, the world often seems overwhelming. So our visits to that little movie house in that town of 2500 souls were rich, indeed, with the things of the human spirit. I remain continually in the debt of those who made me laugh and fantasize then, and since.

Herbert Spencer was a Victorian Age liberal political philosopher. He said that laughter is what he called a "discharge mechanism." Here's a brief statement he made:

"Nervous energy always tends to beget muscular motion. When consciousness is transferred from great things to small, the liberated nerve force will expend itself along the channels of least resistance-muscular movements called laughter."

In other words, laughter is a temporary relief from tension and pressure. Spencer believed that frivolity was necessary in a universe dominated by tooth and claw. And, yes, I know, there are always those only ready and willing to cry out the familiar complaint, "AIN'T IT AWFUL!"

Oscar Wilde was one of the great humorists of the literary world. He was once forced to stand in the pouring rain while being taken to jail. He commented to his jailers, "If this is how her majesty treats her prisoners, she doesn't deserve to have any."

A comedian who I think became a legend in his own time and was to become an excellent dramatic actor in films was George Carlin. He was also a gifted observer of human folly. He suggested why laughter is so important.

When he was growing up he used to look into his bowl of Rice Krispies. "You can't sink them! You try to sink them with a spoon and they come up over the side. I see… that's what fruit is for – it's for sinking the Rice Krispies! A good size peach will down eighty or ninety of them every time. When I'm really mad, I'll drop a cantaloupe on 'em!"

Just let me share a bit more of Carlin's genius. He said in one of his standup shows, "Well, enough about the new sport of indoor hunting. Let me turn to another subject. Names. You know what I'm waiting for? I hope that someday a pope will choose the name 'Buster,' for the Pope. Can't you just see him on the balcony? 'His Holiness, Pope Buster the First.'"

Names are like that. You don't expect certain names among certain groups of people. You *expect* certain things among other groups. You expect certain things when you *hear* certain names. Like you'll know this country is in trouble when we have a president named "Skeeter." When we have a president with a name like "Skeeter" or "Stump" you'll know we have to take time to re-think the whole system.

So, then, if laughter is a safety valve and a reflex action for the overflow of nervous energy, then it is really a justifiable way of coping with tension. As a prisoner in a concentration camp was heard to say. *"I laugh, for if I do not laugh... I will go mad."*

You know, it is also interesting to note that most of today's doctors will agree that a hearty laugh is great exercise. When you emit an explosive laugh, your diaphragm descends, your lungs expand and the amount of oxygen you take in is increased. At the same time, it follows that as the body expands, a kind of gentle massage occurs in the heart and the heart beats faster. Circulation speeds up. And all the time the liver, the stomach and most other of the organs of the body get a kind of invigorating "lift." That is why over 2000 years ago, Aristotle said that "Laughter is a bodily exercise that is precious to one's health."

Another interesting note regarding humor is that many of the theories regarding the presence of it in life evolve out of the tragedy of the human condition. Most of the great humorists led deprived lives or even tortured lives. They were victims themselves, just as were the many figures in the humor they created.

For instance, Charlie Chaplain knew poverty. Lenny Bruce came from a broken home. Allan Sherman was an abused child. George Carlin was a drug user and John Belushi knew mental illness. Of all this, Steve Allen once said, "I have never known a successful comedian who was not somewhat neurotic."

So the humorists seem to have a deep understanding of the tragic in life. Clowns though they be, they are truly acquainted with grief. It must have been true of the genius, Charlie Chaplain. He once said, "The theme of life is conflict and pain. Humor is the subtle discrepancy we understand in what appears to be normal behavior and the antics of the clown. Through humor we see in what seems rational, the irrational; in what seems important, the unimportant. And it also heightens our sense of survival and preserves our sanity. We have to laugh in the face of our helplessness or go insane."

Is it any wonder, then, that so many clowns have not only that look of distressing melancholy, but the haunting appearance of the crucified?

For your enjoyments, I have collected a few intriguing accents on humor. One involves a traveler trying to sneak a bottle of tequila across the border in Laredo, Texas. When the custom official asks what the bottle contains, the traveler replies, "Holy water. It was taken from a religious shrine I visited." The inspector obviously doubts the man's word and opens the bottle. He takes a sip and falls backward. "This is tequila!" he shouts. "Good heavens," cries the traveler, looking up at the sky, "yet another miracle!"

An aged Scotsman, none the worse for wear, staggers home from the pub with a bottle of whiskey in his pocket. A horse drawn carriage comes along and knocks the fellow into a ditch. As he climbs out of the ditch, he feels a wetness flowing down his leg. He looks up to the sky and says, "O God, let it be blood!"

When all is said and done, then, humor struggles in opposition with tragedy. It is the enemy of suffering.

Norman Cousins wrote a bestseller about his illness and titled it *Anatomy of an Illness as Perceived by the Patient*. He was making no progress in getting better while in hospital. So, in cooperation with his physician, he turned to massive doses of Vitamin C, to laughter found in joke books, Marx Brothers' films and other comedic ventures. This became his therapy. He discovered that pain was reduced, that sleep was extended and that inflammation was controlled. In short, he found proof for himself; at least, in the validity of the ancient dictum, "Laughter is good medicine."

I suspect there are many of you here who might be surprised to hear me say that laughter is a tool that can be used for survival. Leaders don't usually encourage laughter. It destroys the impact of propaganda. It ridicules power. It mocks personality. In so many words, it subverts earthly authority and becomes an ally of freedom.

Finally, then, I would be so bold as to suggest that laughter and humor can be seen as religious affirmations. Humor is amusement with life itself. It stands beyond tragedy, symbolically "thumbing its nose" at calamity. In the words of one theologian,

"Laughter is hope's last weapon. In the presence of disaster and death, we laugh instead of crossing ourselves. Or perhaps, better stated, our laughter is our way *of* crossing ourselves. Where laughter and hope have disappeared, humans have ceased to be human."

There are those, I suppose, who would claim that humor is not an appropriate response to conditions in the modern world today. Sober, solemn, dedicated people are unable to look upon life at times as being silly or mundane. They can be atheist or theist, capitalist or socialist, mystic or humanist and there are not just a few in the heady realms of Unitarian Universalism. Reasoned intellect, even nihilism, or, at best, a kind of stoic resignation are their attributes. Tragically, they lack a sense of humor – which can turn about and become a kind of ghastly joke on all concerned.

For me, the presence of humor and laughter in my life is perfectly described in the song by Simon and Garfunkel – a kind of *Bridge over Troubled Waters.*

Levity and wit can be a symbolic "Hand of Life" on the shoulder of the living world often too fragile to continue without it. It can be a method of saving us... from ourselves.

Someone once said to me that it takes half as many muscles to smile as it does to frown. There may be those who prefer the works of Nietzsche or Poe, or even the Apostle Paul who waits for a world to come.

I would cast my vote and place my money on a world in which Mark Twain, the Algonquin Hotel wits and Jackie Gleason comedians try to make us laugh. They are out there working for our sanity. That's where I'd prefer to be... and I think we make more progress toward a better world if we give laughter a chance – just once in a while.

Give this story a chance as I close:

A business sought office help. The sign read: "HELP WANTED. Must be able to type, operate a computer and be bilingual. We are an Equal Opportunity Employer."

A dog trotted up, saw the sign and went inside. He wagged his tail, walked to the sign, looked at it and whined. The officer manager realized the dog was determined and said, "I can't hire you. You can't type." With that the dog went to the typewriter and typed a perfect letter. The manager was stunned. "You also have to be good with the computer." The dog proceeded to enter and execute a perfect program on the computer.

By this time the manager was dumbfounded. "I realize you are intelligent. However, I still can't give you the job." The dog went to the sign about being an Equal Opportunity Employer. "Yes," said the manager, "but it also says you have to be bilingual."

The dog looked at the manager and very calmly said, "MEOW!"

Laughter – "The Sunshine of the Soul."

Amen.

UNIVERSALIST HEROES
AND HEROINES

"Give them, not hell, but hope and courage"
- The Reverend John Murray

To begin this twenty-minute adventure and to set the stage I want to read to you a litany of Universalist names.

Millard Fillmore, American President; Doctor Benjamin Rush, signer of the Declaration of Independence; Hosea Ballou, architect of modern Universalism; The Reverend Thomas Starr King, Universalist minister who saved California for the Union; Mary Livermore, suffragette; P. T. Barnum, showman and originator of "The Greatest Show on Earth" and lifelong member of the Universalist Church in Bridgeport, Connecticut, Owen D. Young, American financier and founder of the Radio Corporation of America.

"Universalism" has been called the biggest word in the language of religion. It is a deep and abiding part of our religious heritage as Unitarian Universalists. Too often I find that my Unitarian Universalist sisters and brothers have not the least in the way of an understanding of Universalism. And so I would like to invite you on this journey of understanding. I hope it will enhance our ability to explain an important aspect of our liberal faith as we seek to grow our denomination.

High above the expanse that makes up the Los Angeles Basin there are wonderful opportunities for mountain drives that overlook the lights of the city. Years ago, during the time in which my parents were discovering Universalism and in the process of becoming early 20th century "come-outers," my father tells the story of an evening upon which he took the family on a drive up into the foothills of Altadena. We had parked there and were observing the twinkling lights of the basin. My brother and I soon went to sleep thus assuring my parents of success in getting us to bed.

137

As Mother and Dad sat there in the quiet of that evening the haggard, troubled face of a young man showed itself in the car window on the driver's side. "Brother, are you saved?" he blurted out. Then he quoted John 3:16: "'that God so loved the world that he gave his only begotten son that whosoever believeth in him would not perish but have everlasting life.'" Then the young man exclaimed again, "Brother, are you saved?"

Very quietly and firmly, my father replied, "Good sir, I am a Universalist. I was never lost!" This left the cocksure young zealot rather speechless. He went wandering down the hill to the next car to try his question again.

My friend and colleague, the Reverend Deane Starr, now deceased and once candidate for President of the UUA, once described his first experience of worship in a Universalist Church. His words are mine, paraphrased from memory.

He said; There I was, burdened with a lifetime of fundamentalist teaching; troubled deeply that I was deserting the faith with my heretical thoughts. And as I sat in that little Universalist Church and heard the words of the minister, I was suddenly charged with excitement. Life was no longer one of continuous gloom. God was not the functionary who merely carried out His threats to all who are born with the sin of Adam upon them. God was immortal, all-caring love among men, women and children. God was there for all of us. We were not lost. We were assured salvation – all people were assured.

And then Deane leaned forward and said to me with sincere intensity:

"Jan, it seemed like I had been shut up in a dark, stifling room all my religious life with no air to breathe. Then, suddenly, it was as if the four walls were in the form of Venetian blinds and someone opened those blinds all at once. And light and fresh, cool pure air flooded my consciousness. I was able to breathe. There was hope. I wasn't lost. And I have never forgotten that wonderful moment. It has stayed with me through a lifetime of liberal ministry."

Something of this kind must have captured the heart and imagination of a young Methodist minister as he sat listening to his friend, James Relly, speak of the unfailing love of God in a world of despair. This new heretical view of God's nature must have made John Murray's spirits rise like Deane Starr's must have. The religious despair in London and throughout Europe in the 18th century was like that.

John Murray, often called the Founder of American Universalism, was born in Alton, England in 1741 and was raised a Methodist. He attended Reverend Whitefield's church for a time, accepting the usual Christian doctrine out of Calvinist teaching. According to that belief, all people are born sinners and need to be saved else they would suffer the eternal fires of damnation in hell. But there was also a catch. Not all people would be chosen by God – only an elected few would enjoy the eternal bliss of heaven. And although you did not know if you would be one of them, failure to accept Jesus Christ as one's Lord and Savior would bring certain doom. One was assured of the irreversible pangs of an eternity of torment where the body is never consumed.

Nonetheless, John Murray was a man unafraid of honest doubt, regardless of the turmoil it brought to his spirit. After a time, he left Reverend Whitefield's church to attend a religious society in Cannon Street, London. There, a certain James Relly, author of a new, heretical book titled *Union*, preached a doctrine of universal salvation. To quote from Murray's autobiography:

"Mr. Relly has said, speaking of the record which God gave of his sin: 'This life is in his Son, and he that believeth not this record, maketh God a liar; it is plain that God hath given this eternal life in the Son to unbelievers, as fully as to believers, else the unbeliever could not, by his unbelief, make God a liar.'" (Murray, *The Life of John Murray*, p. 27)

Slowly but surely, the genius and beauty of this new doctrine wore upon the spiritual consciousness of John Murray. In the little church that he served he began to preach a Gospel of Universalism, much to the displeasure of his hearers. The result was that he lost his position as minister. Being unable to obtain work he could not pay his debts. He was thrown into debtor's prison. While there his beloved wife became seriously ill as did his infant son. With no money or care, they soon died. Upon leaving prison, Murray, understandably grief-stricken and embittered beyond measure, renounced the ministry and refused to practice the Christian faith. He then signed on as a deckhand on the ship *Hand-in-Hand* and set sail for the New World.

It is at this point that Universalist history combines romance and the human tendency to create apocryphal records. Murray, being educated, was quickly given responsible tasks while on board ship. The captain's destination was New York but port regulation kept them from landing there or Philadelphia where they were told they could find harbor. Upon starting back for New York, fog and navigational miscalculations landed them at a place called Cranberry Inlet near Good Luck on New Jersey's south shore.

Murray was put in charge of a small company to go ashore for supplies. The men spread out looking for provisions. Murray noticed a farmhouse not far off and on the way asked a young girl carrying a basket of fishes if he could buy them from her.

"No," she said, "but if you go to that farmhouse there you will get all the supplies you need." With that, she went on.

Sitting on the porch of the old farmhouse was a large, elderly bewhiskered man who introduced himself as Thomas Potter. When Murray replied, Potter said, "I am glad to see you and I have been waiting for you." Thinking this reply somewhat strange, Murray asked why. And it was then that a relationship began that was to change the course of a large portion of American church history forever.

"I have been waiting for a preacher to preach in my meeting house yonder."

Murray looked beyond the old farmhouse to see a tiny white clapboard church. "What do you mean?" asked Murray.

Potter replied, "I have been reading the Holy Scriptures all my life. More and more it has come to me that the gift of life that we are given could not have been from the hands of an angry God as the Reverend Jonathan Edwards insists. It has come to me that God must be a loving kind of God – a father of all creatures. His essence is not anger and hate. It is love. And so I decided that there should be a place in this New World for such a message of hope to be preached. So you see the meeting house I have built with my own hands."

Murray attributed these words to this remarkable man and what follows as well:

"God will send me a preacher, and a very different stamp from those who have heretofore preached in my house. The preachers we have heard are perpetually contradicting themselves, but that God, who has put my heart to build this meeting house will send one who shall deliver unto me his own truth; who shall speak of Jesus Christ and his salvation. My friends often ask, 'Where is the preacher of whom you speak?' And my constant reply has been, 'He will by and by make his appearance.' The moment I beheld your vessel on shore, it seemed as if a voice had audibly sounded in my ears, 'There, Potter, in that vessel... is the preacher you have been so long expecting.'"

Obviously, young Murray was astonished at such words. But on reflection, we must conclude that his speech and civil ways undid him for the educated person he was. In those days, if one was educated, the chances were good that one was at least a teacher, if not a minister. Taking hold of his initial incredulity, Murray asked what might have given Potter the impression he was a preacher. To which Potter replied, "... tis not what I saw, or see, but what I feel, which produces in my mind a full conviction."

Murray: "But my dear sir, you are deceived. I never shall preach in this place, nor anywhere else!"

Potter: "Have you never preached? Can you say that you have never preached?"

Murray: "I cannot. But I never intend to preach again.

Potter: "Has not God lifted up the light of his countenance upon you? Has he not shown you his truth? ...Why should you not show it to others?"

And so the conversation continued with Murray refusing. By this time his men had found him and had been given ample provisions by Potter for the ship's company. Taking leave of his host, Murray thanked him profusely. To which Potter is said to have replied, "The wind will not change, sir, until you have delivered us, in that meeting house, a message from God." (Murray, ibid. p. 139)

One historical account of American Universalist history was written by the Reverend Frederick A. Bisbee in 1920. It was called *From Good Luck to Gloucester*. Bisbee's account of what followed Thomas Potter's pronouncement was almost lyrical in its style.

"Thomas Potter must have been a mystic. He could see the unseen, he could know the unknown. In John Murray, who to his early associates was but a weak sentimentalist, unstable in all his ways, a visionary; Thomas Potter saw the great religious leader who was to rank with Martin Luther as the emancipator of human souls from the thraldom of a cruel and impotent theology, and he held up this man, fleeing from responsibility and service, and challenged him to service... (and) how Murray struggled to escape! But Potter would not let him go until he had delivered the message for which the church had been built, and which was to be the baptism of the renewal of the Gospel of God's Universal Love." (Bisbee, Universalist Publishing House, 1920, p. 31)

And so it was that on September 30, 1770, John Murray preached his first Universalist sermon on the shores of this new land. For the first time, Thomas Potter was to listen to words that he could not only agree with through his study of scripture, but which would comfort his great spirit forever.

Now if you visit the place called Murray Grove on the shore of southern New Jersey, you will find a memorial boulder that was set up and dedicated there in Good Luck in the year 1902. The inscription reads:

"Near this spot first met Thomas Potter, the Prophet, and John Murray, the Apostle of Universalism. The following Sunday, September 30, 1770, in Potter's Meeting House, Murray first preached in America. The wilderness and the solitary place were glad for them."

The record is quite clear from that moment when John Murray went to New York that he began itinerant preaching to those who would listen. Word went out across the land of this young man with a new message of love and hope. It found sympathetic listeners in several families in a place called Gloucester, Massachusetts. That fishing port on Cape Ann north of Boston contained several eminent families who had come across a book brought from England by a young sailor. The book's title was *Union* and its author was none other than the same Reverend James Relly who had preached words of hope to Murray in England years before. Those same families had been meeting to discuss some of the great spiritual insights the book contained and which they felt intuitively themselves.

When word came concerning this new preacher with his message of promise and his emphasis on the universal salvation of all souls with God, it was not long before they brought him to Gloucester to speak. That was in 1774. They wanted to hear for themselves from this man who had been so widely attacked as a "Rellyan" throughout the land. And so, for twenty years, Gloucester became Murray's home. He held his first meeting at the house of Mister Winthrop Sargent, and there met Mister Sargent's widowed daughter, who, in due time, became Mrs. Judith Murray, a woman of marked personal beauty, quick and vigorous intellect, and a partner to her husband's work for all the remaining years of his life.

Judith Murray was but one in a legion of strong and courageous women who came out of the Universalist tradition with a vision of social justice and service to those in need. Scores of projects for social betterment came into being under their direct influence and commitment all around the world. Here, in Europe, in Japan and in the deep South.

So that Judith Murray was one of the first in a growing list of Universalist women whose names have been placed in the halls of American memory for their singular accomplishments for humanity. Clara Barton, founder of the American Red Cross, was a Universalist. The Reverend Olympia Brown was the first woman minister ever to be ordained by a denomination. That was in 1857 and the ordaining body was the Universalist Church of America which John Murray helped to found.

Murray called the Universalists the heralds of universal redemption. This sense of being a part of God's realm of love led Universalists to be in the forefront of efforts to improve the human lot, to transcend the barriers of partialism, to create on earth a foretaste of life in the divine kingdom. It eventually led to the establishment of a denomination that once ranked as the fifth largest membership in the United States. And so the Universalists affirmed "the power of good will and sacrificial spirit to overcome all evil and progressively to establish the Kingdom of God."

Universalists also found little problem in embracing a variety of theological ideas and stances, confident that none of them, however odd or erroneous, could lead to ultimate consequences of unhappiness or damnation. Believe what one would or must, one could not excommunicate oneself from God's love. Among the Universalists were theists, deists, humanists, transcendentalists, yes, even Trinitarians – all with internal variations. Through them all was shown this sense of hope and confidence.

Permit me, then, to bring this brief bit of Universalist history to a close. I have shared this drama if for no other reason than to assure myself that some of you will not only remember, but will retell that same story to others. For it is in the telling of the story that our history is sustained as a liberal religious movement.

The parallels between that time over two centuries ago and the times in which we live, are startling indeed. I need not go into a litany of the several ways in which religion seems to contribute into the pit of fear and superstition. You are as aware as I of some of the outrages committed in the name of religion. Doctrine goes unchallenged. Scripture is studied but never questioned. Millions desert human intellect for the quagmire of religious tyranny.

Equally true were those times in which Murray, Potter, Olympia Brown and Clara Barton lived. Imagine the case with Murray. Here he was, a minister driven from his pulpit for *not* preaching a doctrine of fear; a God of wrath and judgment; an eternal afterlife of burning and suffering in hell. Today, people flock to the magachurches, Bibles in hand, *not* to study and question them, but to accept what they are told – which is *not* to question, only to accept its teachings as inerrant truth.

My prophecy is this. Notwithstanding the fact that we are entering an age of science and technology, of broad-based knowledge and expertise the likes of which the world has never seen, *nevertheless*, more and more people will continue to be more and more frightened as they go through the treadmills of their religious lives. They will be more and more frightened because in the New Testament Book of Revelation it says that when the Millennia arrives, Armageddon will come with it. In the fullness of time, Jesus, the Christ, will return as God's judge to separate people – believers from unbelievers. Those who are not chosen will surely die and will suffer the tortures of hell for eternity.

Mark my words. Millions will hear this message more frequently and with more incessant urging by the preachers of "the Word" than ever before. Who knows what their fear will cause them to do? Who knows to what depths their leaders will go in order to insist on their message?

Considering human behavior today and in the face of this possibility, we as Unitarian Universalists have a unique opportunity, as did John Murray in his time, to become a vanguard for some of those frightened people with an alternative message. A message of hope. A message that contains the simple blessing, belief and promise of a Universal God of Love. These times are similar in many ways to the years in which Murray and Potter lived. People will be hungering for just such a message of joy and compassion.

The Reverend Doctor Gordon "Bucky" McKeeman, my friend, mentor and senior colleague, was for many years Senior Minister of our Unitarian Universalist Church in Akron, Ohio once wrote that:

"As one views the chaotic circumstances of life in the latter part of the twentieth century, it is apparent that hope and confidence, insight and knowledge, courage and commitment are still much needed and may arise from a variety of theological (and philosophical) assertions. The breadth that characterized Universalism from its earliest beginnings seems no less appropriate to the needs of these days. Universalism: for such a time as this."

H. L. Mencken, the remarkable American whose book of quotations is yet to be equaled in comprehensive excellence, was once asked to speak in Topeka, Kansas. He was there to speak in opposition to Prohibition. A woman accosted him as he entered the hall. He invited her to come in to hear him but she said she would only do so if she could make a statement *in favor* of temperance. This she did, asking Mencken what *he* would say if, when he died, he were to be called before Saint Peter and the Heavenly Hosts. Mencken replied, "Madam, I would step forward, bow politely, doff my hat and say, 'GENTLEMAN, I WAS MISTAKEN!'"

I don't know. Perhaps the one true purpose of my life and ministry has been nothing more than to prepare me and others to be strong and courageous for these days. It could be that we have been set apart to answer the message of religious gloom that will surely come as the years continue. But it will take strength, vision and courage to answer such a challenge. For I believe we are again at a threshold where people are ready to hear Murray's words ringing true again, for he said,

"Go out into the highways and byways of America… give the people, blanketed with a decaying and crumbling Calvinism, something of your new vision. You may possess only a small light but uncover it, let it shine, use it in order to bring more light and understanding to the hearts and minds of all. GIVE THEM, NOT HELL, BUT HOPE AND COURAGE! Do not push them deeper into their theological despair, but preach the kindness and everlasting love of God! (Howe, Skinner House Books, 1993, p. 9)

Amen.

[Delivered October 29, 2000, The First Parish, Unitarian in Norwell]

JESUS DID WHAT? – AN EASTER SERMON

On this beautiful day, while hundreds of millions of people the world over celebrate the resurrection of Jesus, who was called "the Christ," many would call us "heretics." We do not believe that bodies rise from the dead – not even Jesus. We fall under the definition of "heretic" since we question the scientific validity of such an assertion.

The price of our heresy, however, is not that expensive. We are protected in our right to disagree. The First Amendment of the Constitution erected a symbolic wall, a "wall of separation" between the religious and the secular. No person or group of people can be set apart and treated differently simply because they hold or do not hold with what has been the majority opinion regarding matters of religion. Our "heresy" is safe.

Unlike the days in Puritan England when Oliver Cromwell and his "Roundheads" ruled from the power of a theocracy, we are granted the right to proclaim our unique perspective without fear of reprisal. However, we must never take such freedom for granted. There will always be those who think they know better what people must proclaim as their religious beliefs.

In the book titled *The Handmaid's Tale*, Margaret Atwood has created a chilling look at what a futuristic world would be like were we to return to the days of Oliver Cromwell. In her earlier works such as *The Edible Woman* and *Surfacing*, Atwood revealed the way women are able to adapt to the exigencies of life.

The Handmaid's Tale is set in the United States in the not-too-far distant future. A bloody governmental *coup d'état* has installed a neo-Puritan dictatorship. The rationale of the governing class – called "the commanders of the faithful" – is religious fundamentalism. Their goal is to make women utterly subservient to the needs of the state. The reason is that society has become threatened with an epidemic of infertility. The reaction to this is to designate any kind of birth control or same-sex relations as crimes punishable by hanging. The highest good is the act of childbearing. Every woman is assigned to one of several specific roles, depending upon what is referred to as her "fertility quotient."

What's more remarkable is how clearly Ms. Atwood supports the thesis of her novel by using facts out of contemporary conditions. At the time of its writing, for instance, there were bills before several state legislatures requiring women to get consent of their nearest *male relative* before having an abortion. In Scandinavia, birth rates have fallen precipitously over the past few decades. In Rumania, laws were once passed prohibiting abortion and birth control. Under the dictatorship of Nicolae Ceausescu, monthly pregnancy tests were compulsory – and that is a fact. In 1996, on a trip to Transylvania to make contact with my former church's partner congregation, my interpreter, a student of history at the University, affirmed it.

The annals of the past prove, then, that no group can ever afford to be sanguine regarding the continuance of religious or civil freedom, no matter what tradition holds.

This is a difficult time for many Unitarian Universalists. There are many of our fellow Unitarian Universalists who have left orthodox Christianity behind, having rejected a faith system that requires belief in the unbelievable.

This does not solve our problem, however. Many other Unitarian Universalists are quite comfortable in affirming the ties we have with the Judeo-Christian tradition. Their quest for truth prevents them from totally accepting the stories surrounding the Easter myth. But they sense that there is some merit in learning what the symbols surrounding the legend might teach. They do not wish to be those who "throw the baby out with the bath."

This is what makes us the diverse religious association we have become. The tension is always there. There are probably not a few who, out of respect for the religious tradition of some family member, have not attended an orthodox Protestant or even Roman Catholic service at Easter; who have not heard people talking about "the *actual events* that happened after Jesus died on the cross." Such literal interpretations are troubling, though, even when beloved family members proclaim them.

Unitarian Universalists accept nothing of the literal meaning of the Easter story. But we are also vigilant to protect the rights of others to so believe. That is what religious freedom is all about. Religions have the right to coexist, no matter how they differ.

Some folks don't see it that way. A literal interpretation of the Bible would *insist* that all who hear the "good news" of the Resurrection must believe as a little child accepts the teachings of its parents.

So it makes it even more difficult for us as Unitarian Universalists. While we want to protect the rights of others and to be tolerant of that with which we disagree, we are sometimes placed in the uncomfortable position of being told "theirs" is the only way. Failure to accept it will sink the world into interminable darkness.

Permit a personal reflection of this. It was the year of the Republican Convention in Houston. I happened at that time to be the Chairman of the Religious Issues Committee of Planned Parenthood of Houston. We knew that Randall Terry and those of his following were planning to picket the eleven Planned Parenthood Clinics throughout the city. Care was taken to plan ways of insuring that those clinics would remain open. And so, on opening day of the convention, Lorna and I and our two younger daughters showed up at the main downtown clinic – at five in the morning. We established an actual human wall of people around the entries to the clinic. Then, at about seven that same morning, hundreds of what I can only assume were sincere and dedicated Christians began to align themselves across the street from us. It was not long before their leaders began to incite them to such heights that they were soon standing face-to-face with us, proclaiming "the word of the Lord," holding Bibles in the air, shouting at us, yelling their dictates, demanding we disperse and the clinic close. Posters and models of fetuses were everywhere. Mothers with small children screamed at us while their sons and daughters looked up into their parents' angry faces. On and on it went until a courageous judge evoked a restraining order making it a felony to be less than one hundred feet from any Houston clinic. But you could feel the power of unexamined religious zeal. It was palpable.

Henry Nelson Wieman was one of the most prominent mid-twentieth century Unitarian Universalist theologians. He held the chair of theology at the University of Chicago for many years. He once wrote:

There is a fairly pernicious feature in the degeneration of religion. The immediate objective in any social enterprise always involves a stand in relation to persons, for and against. When the horizons of our religion narrow themselves down to some one specifically formulated objective, all the driving power of our religious loyalty may become focused upon persons – for some and against others. Then the persons who are opposed to us cease to be human in our eyes. They become devils. They become the incarnation of all that is obstructive to the forward movement of history and the fulfillment of highest values.

(Wieman, *Source of Human Good*, pg. 67)

It is not surprising, then, to find religious pressure groups acting under the legitimate protection of the Bill of Rights, to pressure various presidents into positions regarding prayer in the public schools, abortion, the alteration of textbooks to religiously "acceptable" teachings such as creationism and other matters affecting the body politic. How well I recall our sadness in seeing the Equal Rights Amendment fail by two ratifying states. Religious pressure had prevailed.

Over the past few years I have found in the Southwest, where the Knosts have lived for over a decade that it has become quite unpopular to be known either as a "liberal" or as a "religious humanist." I assume that to be true in the great Southeast as well. But take heart. It is a choice we Unitarian Universalists have made and one of which we should be proud.

Today, for instance, we remember the Easter story. The power of that story is very real for millions. However, as Unitarian Universalists, we take a few steps further than mute acceptance of what cannot be proven.

The story tells of a man – a man – who was arrested by the Roman authorities for acts in opposition to the established order in Jerusalem. The story tells of the fact that when that man was questioned he would not say one word in his defense. His people – followers included – were confused. Some expected him to be a strong deliverer – a Messiah who would lead them, as Moses did, away from the bondage of pagan Rome.

But he would have no part of such a role. And it is difficult to imagine what he may have been thinking. Certainly he had his doubts about whether he would succeed in his mission. He even pleaded in his prayers that some sign be given him so that a clearer answer would be there for him – to continue or to leave Jerusalem. The story also tells of a supper he observes with his disciples, of his strangely accurate prediction of his betrayal and of his final judgment.

When pronounced guilty of treason, he was driven with whips and cudgels to a hill called Calvary. He was made to carry a crude wooden cross all the way. The record tells of the horrible custom of actually nailing a human being to a cross with great spikes through the hands and feet and of setting it in the ground so that the victim died by a combination of bleeding to death and by suffocation, hanging thus.

It is with astonishment that we learn, notwithstanding the cruel picture thus related, that the Easter story is one of hope. Strange. But we find that the reason it is thought of in that way is that something unprecedented seemed to take place in the minds of Jesus' followers since after three days in which his body had been placed in a tomb – they couldn't find it. And then some began saying that they had experienced signs of his return – over and over. And people began to believe he had pulled it off – that he had kept his word and cheated the grave.

This is the story that millions – I say hundreds of millions – accept each Easter as the unadulterated truth behind all other truths. And so it is… for them…

Easter's dichotomy for us as Unitarian Universalists, then, is the wide divergence between our complete rejection of anything like the superstitious elements of the story of Jesus, his life, death and supposed resurrection. But we are hard-pressed to reject all the elements of the religious perspective this man brought with his life and example.

The world today viewed through the eyes of the pessimist is a dark world, isn't it? People are still starving. Natural cataclysms like tornadoes kill scores of innocent people almost without warning. Adolescents take guns into their hands and kill their classmates and teachers. People are tortured. But wait.

Perhaps we are missing something. There have been marvelous occurrences, too. We need to remember human victories, as well. Because usually the theme of Easter has been one of death denial. It speaks usually about the resurrection of the dead, of the triumph of life over death. But there are some facts to warrant it.

Were Jesus to live today, there is no doubt that he would be an outspoken spearhead for social reform for the poor. He would be opposed to any kind of arms race. Were he alive in Bosnia, he would be calling down judgment on the war criminals there. Were he alive in Northern Ireland he would be picketing outside the building where the peace accords are being discussed. Were he alive in the Middle East he would be calling the judgment of God down on the heads of state of Israel *and* the Palestinians. Were he alive in India and Pakistan he would echo the words of love and peace that Gandhi taught. He would most likely be on the capitol steps in Baghdad or the capitol in Libya calling judgment on Saddam Hussein or Moammar Gaddafi for as long as he was allowed to speak – which wouldn't be long.

And… and… were he alive anywhere where assault weapons and killing weapons of any kind – he would be protesting their use. As a matter of fact, notwithstanding the way he died, he would most probably be over at the penitentiary protesting the use of the death penalty as a symbol of public revenge. O yes, he would be here among us.

And do you know what? HE WOULD BE A TOTALLY UNACCEPTTABLE PUBLIC FIGURE, DERANGED IN THE EXTREME.

So here we are with our tension between the beauty of the resurrected natural world and our rejection of the resurrection story – caught on the hinges of a dilemma between finding meaning in life and coming to our eventual death tragically having never found a way to find a way to make our lives count.

To lay down one's life for a cause one feels deeply and believes in is one thing; to give up one's life without reason is another. And to come to death realizing that one never did really live is still another – and perhaps for some a commonplace occurrence.

So again we are placed right in the middle of that wonderful dilemma which Easter and the Springtime bring. And I would rather be there, twisting in the tension of that dichotomy than to ignore the depth of life's reality and when I come to the end of my life discover that I had never lived.

I want to close with a poem by Robinson Jeffers that is timely and accurate for our day:

(Here was read the poem "The Answer" by Robinson Jeffers)

Welcome to the enigma of being alive, a wondrous season not of dark and dread, but of light and hope as well!

Happy Easter, Happy Springtime!

Amen.

BEDSIDE MANNERS

> … Wait… and keep awake with me.
>
> Matthew 26:37

It has oft been said that the most important task a congregation has is that of being a continuing community. By this I mean that each person who is a part of this family has a responsibility to be more than a sponge; taking from this experience, learning from that discussion, being moved by such and such a service of worship, or being inspired by a particular sermon

One can say "People, be good," and, indeed, in their hearts, they ARE mostly good. But the business of "doing good" often is threatening or fearful. This is not caused by any sense of ill-being in the person. Mostly, it emanates from our sense of inadequacy; or not knowing just "how" to reach out, to care, to be of assistance. And so, as a parallel, one of the most important tasks of any spiritual leader of a congregation is to provide insight, ideas, suggestions, and assistance in this realm.

This morning, I want to talk about the ominous necessity all of us face, from time to time, of being with sick persons, whether in a hospital or home setting. I also wish to allude, to a lesser degree, but certainly just as firmly, to the ways we often fail to be a "cup of strength" to someone who is presently or has just recently lived through some personal loss or other tragedy. You might call this one of my "How To Do It" series. But it is an important matter for us to consider if we mean it when we say we want to become more of a community.

So many times, in reaching for some beginning illustration of what one wishes to say, it is found powerfully recounted in some passage of Scripture. How true this is of the reading this morning! Here was a man called Jesus, deeply saddened by the knowledge that what his life had served was about to come apart at the seams. No one had understood him – least of all his faithful disciples. Here he was talking about a kingdom of the heart – a kingdom of love and forgiveness – a way of traveling through this life – and they were sitting around thinking what a great day it would be when he finally admitted that he was to be the stalwart, dashing, and assertive Messiah – the anointed one, the Conqueror, who would rid their lives of the Roman oppressors in revolution and rebellion.

And so Jesus, feeling this depression of spirit, went out to a place called the Garden of Gethsemane "to pray" as the account has it, perhaps to meditate, to center himself, to quiet his fears and calm himself to the inevitable which must come if he was to be true to his reason for being. And he asked that three of his followers, Peter and the two sons of Zebedee, wait for him while he went a little way off to think alone. He asked of them a simple request. "Wait here and watch with me." And each time he came back, he found them asleep. Now many have studied this story. There have been many theories for why he asked that they stay awake. Could it have been to warn him of impending danger? No. He knew sooner or later the authorities would come. Could it be that he was lonely and wanted their company? No. He wanted solitude. Could it have been that he was afraid of the dark? Probably not. It probably was his need to know that three of his companions would be "with him in his pain and suffering." His hope was that they understood his confusion, his doubt, his sense of loss and that they could simply support him with their silence and their presence.

What additional suffering he must have felt when he returned those three times to find them, true to their humanism, sleeping in the night. "The spirit indeed is willing, but the flesh is weak."

Surely there have been times when you have wanted out of some situation in which you are called to be "with" a person who is ill or dying. The reasons for such discomfiture are obvious. Being ill is not the norm. The norm is health, youth, vitality, being alive. When the bodily or mental functions have rendered someone unable to meet such expectations, they become "not normal," and we tend to shy away.

Why? Perhaps the principle reason is that we don't know what to say… or do… under such circumstances. We are afraid we'll "blow it" and do something inappropriate or unkind. Indeed, we might even feel that we could cause additional harm by our presence – or make ourselves believe such a tempting escape – and so we don't do anything. And in that failure to respond, the community shrivels a little. The dream of community dims a little.

Let me, then, presume to make some suggestions that will aid you in being effective in such cases. Much of what I am about to say takes the form of common sense, but it needs repeating because we tend to lose sight of the principles upon which such caring is built.

It is one thing to have a member of one's family in the hospital. It is not difficult for us to energize our resources and go to the aid of a loved one. No requests are too much; no hours too long when we are prayerfully working and waiting for a loved one to return to health.

But suppose it is someone NOT of our family. Suppose it is someone we don't know very well or with whom we have but a passing acquaintance. That's when the nervousness starts to set it. That's when we start to become very busy and just don't manage to get over to the nursing home or up to the hospital to see them. What to do?

First of all, prepare. Personally and informationally. You are about to be with a person who is ill. Two things have to happen. One is that you must divest your mind of all extra baggage that will get in the way of an authentic meeting. The preparation for being with another involves a kind of cleansing of the mind of incidentals, unimportant and irrelevant observations. Create, as it were, a *tabula rasa*, a "blank slate." You are going to try, so far as you can, to affirm the person you are about to visit – so you do not want to be the star, or let your own personality get in the way of their needs. Secondly, in preparation, it doesn't hurt to stop at the desk or speak to a nurse about it. For instance,

"Nurse, I am about to go visit Mr. B down in room 222. I want to be of any support I can. Is there anything I should know? What's the best thing I can do?"

Usually, if they are not being overworked as is so often the case, the nurses will give as much information as they feel you need to be effective. They are not going to violate the codes of confidentiality or good taste, but they could say something like:

"Of course. Mr. B has had kind of a bad night, and you might find him dozing. But I am sure he will be delighted to see you. You can gently waken him if he is asleep. It is really good for him to be able to talk with someone. But don't stay too long."

This gives you a little presence of mind and intentionality as you enter the room. If the door is closed, you know that a nurse or doctor is with the patient, and so you must BE patient and wait until it is appropriate to enter. Then comes the most important thing you can be or do.

What you must try to do in affirming this person is to give him control of the visit where you can. One way is to say something like, "Look, you tell me when this visit needs to be over." You might say, "I'll plan to stay for fifteen minutes, but if it is too tiring, you let me know." Many times, patients will say, "Oh, stay as long as you want," when they don't really mean it but would rather be uncomfortable or even suffering rather than embarrass someone who has taken the trouble to be with them. So that sense of timing has to come from you – and you have to try to let them take the lead.

Another thing. And this is paramount. THE SHORTER TIME THAT YOU ARE WITH A PERSON, THE MORE IMPORTANT IT IS THAT YOU SHOULD SIT DOWN! Sitting down makes a difference. Oh, I know, a lot of people don't take the trouble to ask, "Can I pull up a chair?" because they like to feel that the patient can look up to their faces without having to twist and turn to see them. But, friends, even a person in a body cast can look with his eyes and not have to twist all around to see us. Sitting down means you are intending to be "with them" and not just standing there waiting for the first opportunity to skip out.

As a matter of fact, in talking with some of my colleagues at Overlook Hospital, I found that a study had been done (I do not have the specific documentation), in which five doctors visited five patients standing… and then they visited with five other patients while seated. The first group remembered, when asked, that their doctor had been with them maybe three or four minutes. The second group confidently assured the questioner that the doctor had been with them seven or eight minutes that day. Being seated makes a difference.

There are some helpful leading questions that you can use to get "into" the visit.

"How do you feel?"

Such a question alludes to the physical side of the situation and allows the patient to take the lead and share what they will of their condition.

"How is it going?" or *"How are you doing?"*

156

or even *"How's it been?"*

These are questions that lead into the emotive or the spiritual side of a person's condition, and they can take the lead appropriately or not.

Even such a question as, "How are your spirits today?" can allow the person asked to take the answer in either direction.

Of course, there are some questions that are emphatically NOT helpful. Those that contain sarcasm or humor mask our nervousness and belittle what is obviously a troubling scenario for the person jibed or joked. Bedpan humor is unnecessary and counterproductive. It is often a way for the visitor to mask his anger with the situation, and it skews the visit: it brings it over to the visitor's control. In other words, such *ripostes* say nothing more than "I want you to joke with me about being here." The television set is on. Scrambling for something to say, we mumble, "What have you been watching lately?" Not helpful. If you are a family member, it is okay because you are there a lot more and they understand. But the distance that is created by such questions makes it impossible for you as a visitor to be of support as you really intend.

In working with seminary students who have been interns under my supervision in other churches, I have always described this process as the difference between BEING and DOING. "Doing for" and "Being with." "How are you?" can either be a problem for a patient to answer... Or it can be an excellent lead into a wider sharing in which the patient is affirmed and made whole.

I can remember two stories, one fanciful, the other actual, which illustrate inappropriate activity on the part of the questioner. The first is the story of the minister who bounds into the hospital room, all sunshine and roses, and proceeds to laugh and joke and say what a wonderful day it is outside without so much as a pause to let the patient take the lead. When he notices that the patient is struggling for breath inside his oxygen tent, he reaches in and hands him a pencil and notebook to WRITE DOWN what he wants to say to the minister. The patient laboriously scribbles a message – then faints. The nurse rushes in on hearing the excited cries of the former "sunshine fellow" and reads the note. She looks at the insensitive, confused cleric and says, disgustedly, "Reverend, the note says, 'You're standing on my OXYGEN HOSE!'"

The other story is one I might have mentioned to some of you. It happened while I was chaplain trainee in my Clinical Pastoral Education program at Boston State Mental Hospital back in 1959. I was a resident chaplain and so each morning would go through the line at the cafeteria where dollops of powdered eggs and sausage which tasted man-made were dumped onto my plate alongside the rolls that would cleave to the insides like so much cement. There was a patient who had been given the freedom of the grounds and simple duties to perform prior to being released from the hospital. His name was Harold. I would see him every morning as he dolefully spooned this goop onto the proffered plates. One sunny hot Boston morning, as I moved through the line, I said, "Good morning, Harold, how are you?" He fixed me with a steely gaze and shouted, "You don't mean that!"

I never felt so foolish. I wanted to undo the words, but they stood as spoken. I have never forgotten, nor do I ever try to ask such a question of someone without meaning to listen to his or her answer – whether it takes twenty minutes or not.

People in hospitals many times are scared. Like Jesus, who was probably queasy and frightened at the unknown that he was about to face, hospital patients might very well ask, "Why is this happening to me?" Of course, this is more of a problem for the clergy because, presumably, we are supposed to have answers to such questions. We have seminary training, we are experienced and read a lot, we are representative of a congregation and the religious side of life, but we don't have the answers, either.

James Michener in his wonderful book *Hawaii* alludes to this "asking" in the passage we have read this morning. The people, in their grief at the dying of their queen, kept repeating over and over, "Au-ee! Au-ee!" It is a cry of grief, a chant of asking, a "We, we!" A "Why? Why?" It is an expression of pain – and it is a medium in which pain and sadness can come out. "Oi! Vey!" at the Wailing Wall. And in the hospital room. "Why me? Why this? Why?" We haven't the answer, but we are with them. And so, in our ambivalence, our reluctance to say or do anything, we are silent. And even in that, we are of great assistance.

We can listen.

We can be with them.

We can let them set the pace... insofar as they can... without preaching, with foggy-minded, pie-in-the-sky Pollyanna-isms.

One last thing about hospital calling. The matter of touch. How important it is for us to realize that to touch someone, caringly and soothingly, means a great deal. Consider. A hospital is one place in which no one usually touches us except to inflict some kind of pain or discomfort. There are shots – the needles. The poking and prodding: "Does this hurt?" There are all manner of circumstances in the patient's care that necessitate a certain amount of pain being brought into the picture.

But what about a simple touch? A reaching of the hand, even a holding of the hand? Does this bring pain? On the contrary, it is the warm contact with another human being who wishes deeply for that sick person's recovery, physically and spiritually. There is a marvelous woodcut that was done by the artist Albrecht Durer which depicts Jesus reaching into the pit of hell to comfort the souls who have been put there. All around are the incubi and succubae of the devil. In the heavens, shining above, are the angels and cherubim singing their hearts out. But here is Jesus, a human being, a man, standing before this window, as it appears, and there are three or four hollow-eyed, suffering persons below him. He is not speaking. He is not trying to lift them out. He is merely extending his hand. And they are in the process of reaching up to the assurance of that extended caring hand.

Our hands, at the end of extended arms, are the physical testament we can give to others of what is surely in our minds and hearts for them – true caring – true "concern" and willingness to risk beyond mere words and show that we are "with them" in their present condition.

A young man named Jim had contracted a viral paralysis called *Gianberee* (a physician can correct my pronunciation). This is a disease where one is completely unable to move. And the chaplain came in for a visit. He sat down, took Jim's hand and said, "How do you feel?" and Jim was unable to reply except with two blinks for "Yes" and one blink of the eyes for "No." "Does my holding your hand bother you?" One blink. "Is it all right if I continue it?" Two blinks. After the visit, the chaplain went to the nurse and suggested that when the mother and the wife of Jim came in that they begin to stroke his arms to give him some monitoring of himself – so that he could feel "existence." Jim was cured. And when he saw the chaplain, he said, "You know, when you first took my hand, I had been feeling like a bag of worms. Here were all these nerve endings with no messages to send back to my brain. It was driving me crazy. But the touch that I received from you – and from my wife and my mother, the two of them, around the clock, kept me from going insane. I thank you for your touch."

I would like to share a story, also from Scripture, that will, I think, sum it all up. In fact, this story also alludes to ways in which we can be with others in their time of tragedy as well as in a hospital setting. It reads:

"The news of all the disasters that had fallen on Job came to the ears of three of his friends. Each of them set out from home – Eliphaz of Teman, Bildad of Shuah and Zophar of Naamath – and by common consent they decided to go and offer him sympathy and consolation. Looking at him from a distance, they could not recognize him; they wept aloud and tore their garments and threw dust over their heads. They sat there on the ground beside him for seven days and seven nights. To Job they spoke never a word, so sad a sight he made."

Job 2:11-12 (*Jerusalem Bible*, P. 632)

My friends, if we are to become more than a diverse group of interesting people who gather once a week to sing, meditate, and listen; if we are to become more than a scattered community separated by many cities and towns who gravitate to this free religious community for insight and spiritual fulfillment, then we must find ways of reaching others than ourselves and our families. As you closed your eyes this morning, in the directed meditation that we shared, you MUST have felt the warmth and presence of other human beings, caring human beings, who WANT TO BE MORE THAN JUST SPONGES, but rather ministers to each other. And if we can do this, more and more, among ourselves, and with those strangers who enter our quest in search of the religious life fulfilled, then we cannot fail to be a cup of strength, a beacon of caring situated on this little corner in this little town.

I ask you to join me in that reaching, that commitment to caring, that mission of good fulfilled: BEING WITH and DOING FOR others than our own small circle of life.

When it begins to happen, all the problems, all the afflictions of the spirit, all the confusions and doubts that we have about the reason for our being will melt as ice in the sun, and we will have that sense of family devoutly to be wished.

I want to close with a very familiar passage used many times at the opening of our services. I ask you to let these words mean more than the surface hearing would imply – to the depth of the spirit that is in each of us as we share this gift of life and caring with others in community, our community.

> We arrive out of many singular rooms, walking the
> branching streets.
> We come to be assured that our brothers and sisters
> surround us, to restore their images on our eyes.
> We enlarge our voices in common speaking, and
> singing.
> We try again for that solitude found in the midst of
> those who with us seek THEIR hidden reckonings.
> Our eyes reclaim the remembered faces; their voices
> stir the surrounding air.
> The warmth of their hands assures us, and the glad-
> ness of our spoken names.
> This is the reason of cities, of homes, of assemblies
> in the houses of worship and fellowship.
> It is good to be, once again, with one another.
>
> - Kenneth Patton (Paraphrased by J.V.K.)

UTRIM SIT DEUS?

(IS THERE A GOD?)
Utrum sit Deus? Videtur quod non. – St. Thomas Aquinas

The question we are considering today is not new. It may fairly be deemed a perennial question. The Latin quotation which I just shared appeared in one of the greatest theological works of all time. It was called the *Summa Theologica* and was written over 600 years ago by Saint Thomas Aquinas. "*Utrum sit Deus?*" (Is there a God?) "*Videtur quad non.*" (It seems not.)

It is difficult to believe that one of the greatest Roman Catholic theologians would answer the question in such a way. But he did it with a purpose. He wrote the question in that way in order to set up an opportunity to argue several other reasons *for* the existence of God. Here's a close approximation of his words:

"... everything that is... has some reason for being. In a world of time-limited, non-necessary beings, some of which explain the existence of others, *ultimately*, at the end of the chain of causes, there has to be a *being* that needs no explanation. This being must be infinite – that is, defying the limits of time. It must be eternal – that is, never-ending. It must be a necessary being and the only possible explanation for a world *full* of beings that are finite, temporal and contingent..."

This may be one of the great arguments of theological history with respect to the question of the existence of God. I will admit that it requires a metaphysical line of thinking and I realize such thinking is none-too-popular in today's world. And yet, Aquinas was not alone. Others support his point.

Voltaire, that indomitable French author and philosopher of the Enlightenment once stated in a letter to Emperor Frederick the Great that:

"My reason tells me that God exists, but it also tells me that I can never know what God is."

Jonathan Edwards, the great American preacher and reformer was quite convinced of the nature of deity as he stated in his sermon, "Sinners in the Hands of an Angry God":

"The God that holds you over the pit of Hell, much as one holds a spider... over the fire, abhors you... His wrath toward you burns like fire; He looks upon you as worthy of nothing else but to be cast into the fire; He is of purer eyes than to bear to have you in His sight; you are ten thousand times more abominable in His eyes than the most hateful, venomous serpent is in ours."

Fifty years later, a British radical by the name of Tom Paine wrote a book to defend his belief in deism. Paine was a singular initiator of many of the ideals of the American Revolution. In his essay *The Age of Reason*, he observed that:

"The only idea one can affix to the name of God is that of a first cause, the cause of all things. Incomprehensible and difficult as it is for a person to conceive what a first cause is, one arrives at the belief of it from the tenfold difficulty of disbelieving it."

Even Origen, the early Christian father remembered for his departure from mainline Catholicism in his radical embrace of the concept of universal salvation, was careful in his description of what he meant by the word "God":

"God must not be thought of as a physical being or as having any kind of body. God is pure mind. God moves and acts without needing any corporeal space, size, or form, or color, or any other property of matter."

It would seem, though, that our modern world is quicker to recognize passing impressions and feelings than it is to consider eternal questions propounded by ancient sages. For instance, Anselm was said to have been the greatest thinker ever to adorn the throne at Canterbury Cathedral. He was often called "the second Augustine." He, too, wrestled with this problem. Perhaps his greatest contribution to this continuing dialog was his *Ontological Proof of God*:

"We define God as that being than whom none greater can be conceived. But if such a being existed only in the intellect, it would not be the absolute greatest, for we could add a greater existence in reality. It follows, then, that the original concept – God- exists *not* in the mind but in a larger reality…"

The matter of whether one believes in some form of being or existence beyond the limits of human experience does not depend upon Thomas Aquinas and his power to convince, any more than to take the more philosophical approach of a great thinker like Anselm.

Each of us has his or her arguments for or against the existence of some transcendent being. The fact of the matter is that humanity has *always* had an innate perception of God – or the lack thereof. A person's understanding of whether there is a God or not is tied with some of the deepest strains of consciousness.

Most men and women seek "the good" in their lives. Despite false starts, endless failing and the cynical denial of hope, people tend to work to that end; that is, to the accomplishment of "what is good" in life.

In our solitude we may find ourselves asking, "What it is all about?" "Who am I?" "How did I come to be here?" "Where am I going?" We hear a newborn baby's cry or, more wonderfully, witness the birth of a baby; or we stare in wonder into the massive reaches of space; we stand motionless watching a beautiful bird or know the joy of autumn's incredible colors. In any of these we are no different than those of time previous who wondered and wandered in the same universe of thought.

Even in the darkness of lost hope when people war upon one another, killing and being killed, or committing unspeakably cruel acts in the name of their selfish interest, even then, as the German theologian, Dietrich Bonhoeffer, affirmed in the death camp: "The thought of God is witnessed in the dark night when one is most alone."

"Who am I?" "Where was I before my knowledge of this world?" "Where am I going?"

Let me share the way one man approached these questions. He was once a Missouri farm boy. Today, he is ranked with names like Galileo, Newton and Einstein. He was one of the greatest scientists in history. His name was Harlow Shapley and he was an astrophysicist. He often said of his work that "he liked to look through the windows of the Milky Way… and beyond."

Someone once kidded him by asking if there was any milk in the Milky Way. He replied, "Of course, and they're one of my favorite brands of candy!" Shapley had an innate sense of wonder and a wish for world unity. It made him larger than life. Some have opined that Shapley was a spiritualist of sorts. One wonders at such an unlikely prospect. Why? Consider. He once wrote the following:

"I… am a pretty good operator with a forked twig. Once I had a dousing twig cut under a waxing moon from an apple tree growing beside a graveyard. (Ed. Note: all the ingredients necessary for a stick that "finds water.") It was supersensitive; it ignored the nearby Charles River but it located a pint of bourbon in a friend's hip pocket!"

In his later years, Doctor Shapley wrote a number of books in addition to those he wrote on the subject of astronomy. Two were titled *Science Ponders Religion* and *The Scientist Speculates*. In them, he talked about the possibility that the sky must contain not only the stars we see glowing, but dark ones we cannot see.

Doctor Shapley also founded a magazine called *Science News* and was a frequent speaker at Unitarian Universalist Summer Institutes. One explanation of his reasoning was an explanation of Fuller's Equation: "1 + 2 = 4." Odd? Not at all. If you take one equilateral triangle and add two more in a pyramid, you form a fourth triangle in the middle.

Shapely described this as an example of the whole being greater than the sum of its parts. He even suggested that it might explain the creation of oceans. If you add one atom of oxygen to two atoms of hydrogen, you create something more than these two invisible gasses.

In the 17th century, Lord Orrery of Northern England ordered a model of the solar system constructed for his gardens. It was a marvelous piece of machinery. It was constructed in total keeping with Kepler's discoveries. There was a brass sun and globes that represented the planets which revolved around it. Lord Orrery had a friend who was an outspoken atheist. He came to the castle to see this new invention.

"Who made it?" he asked.

"Nobody made it… it just happened," answered Lord Orrery.

"How could that be? I don't believe it. These intricate gears and wheels couldn't just create themselves. Who made them?"

Lord Orrery kept insisting that it just happened. The atheist friend rapidly worked himself into a snit of hysterical frustration.

Finally, Orrery said, "I was just testing you. Now... I will offer you a bargain. I will promise to tell you truly who made my little 'solar system' here in my garden as soon *as you tell me truly who made the infinitely better, more wonderful, more beautiful sun and planets there in the heavens!*"

His friend turned pale. For the first time he realized that there existed the possibility that the universe might be more than impersonal, neutral and non-random. Orrery's theorem, then, states that:

If the model of any natural system requires intelligence for its creation and its working, the natural system itself requires at least as much intelligence for its own creation and working.

We must be careful, however, in stating that Orrery's theorem is not a proof of the existence of God. Lucretius was a Roman poet who wrote well over 2000 years ago. His six-part poem, "*De Rerum Natura*," is written in the form of a dialog between Lucretius and Democritus.

In the dialog, they talk about the grains of sand on the beach, hardly indistinguishable one from the other at a distance of ten feet. One suggests that perhaps the sea is made of such invisible grains. The exchange proceeds until Lucretius comes to the conclusion that one of the most beautiful experiences a person can have is to comprehend the mystery that is beyond one's comprehension. As a matter of fact, the passage engraved on the gravestone of Harlow Shapley was chosen by him as it appeared in the works of Lucretius. But even there, Lucretius admitted that it had been written down many years before he lived and he was simply quoting it. It read:

"One man ventured far out beyond the flaming ramparts of the world and voyaged in mind throughout eternity, returning victorious. He proclaimed to us what be and what cannot... and we, by his triumph, are lifted level with the skies."

Perhaps you've wondered, as I have, whether some intelligence observes us as some grand experiment. Does the research biologist feel that the same right he or she assumes in experimentation with large numbers of laboratory animals may also apply to some sort of super-intelligence unknown to us but using us for a similar purpose?

Every race of humanity has recognized some sort of mystic force and has attributed power to many varied phenomenon; the sun, the moon, the stars, thunder and lightning, volcanoes or some living creature.

Pygmies in Central Africa commune with their nightly chants of devotion. They explain that they cannot see any god while alive, so they have no idea what form god takes. They also know that such a god is wise and good because they are given everything they need. They are confident that spirit is of the forest where they live. So they sing to the forest and listen reverently for whatever whispers come to their hearts in reply.

I am sure most of you remember the movie *The Gods Must Be Crazy*. It was actually more than an excellent comedy. It was also a commentary on the hope that there still remain those of a simpler nature in this world who are unspoiled by what the columnist, Walter Lippmann, once termed "the acids of modernity." The "bushmen" of the Kalahari Desert say to us, in so many words:

"There is a great dream across the world that we are part of. It is not like any ordinary dream in sleep. For we do not dream this dream. Instead, this dream dreams us. It dreams us all the time, even while we are awake, and we know that it must be lived out on this earth, through everything we do."

These concepts seem disconnected, I know. They come as if from two boughs of the same tree of human experience. One is the widespread parallel religious teachings of such major prophets of the race as Krishna, Zoroaster, Buddha, Moses, Jesus, Mohammed, Gandhi, Teresa and King.

Each figure is unique in place and time – but the differences that stemmed from such sages were only picked up by their followers, never by them. The first bough of this imaginary tree, then, is the bough of religious parallels.

The other bough spreads into the parallel of scientific teaching and discovery. Great teachers such as Aristotle, Ptolemy, Copernicus, Kepler, Galileo, Newton, Shapley, Curie, Fuller and Einstein make up that list. Theirs was a natural progression of evolving thought. Each built on the shoulders of the other.

Now... look again at the religious bough. Try, with me, to see it, not as a story of opposing principles in confrontation – but as connected boughs stemming from the same trunk of Life. The harmony of thought shared by these great souls rested ultimately with much the same thoughts, ideas and transcendent realities no matter what they called the: Jehovah – God – Allah – Great Spirit – The Force – Spirit of Life, Scientific Method or Cosmic Design.

They are no more or less enemies of each other than was Ptolemy toward Copernicus or Einstein was jealous of Galileo or Newton. Correct me if I am wrong, but I have been hard-pressed to find any example of the Buddha denying Krishna or of Jesus opposing Moses or striking down the Ten Commandments. On the contrary, it was Jesus who said very clearly that "I came not to destroy the law and the prophets, but to fulfill them."

Over the years I've had occasion to know and talk with people who embrace the Baha'i faith system. One of their teachings is shared in our liberal religious tradition. Baha'ists believe that everyone is entitled to his or her own investigation of the truth. This leads to the essential harmonization of science and religion. Baha'i's founder, Baha'u'llah once wrote:

"Science and religion are as the two wings of a bird. The bird is (human)kind, which cannot fly on one wing alone. For the wing of science, if it lacks the insight of religion to balance it, leads to materialism. And the wing of religion, unguided by the reasonableness of science, leads to superstition."

There is no doubt that many of the scientific world would insist that the criterion of human experience is infinitely superior to what might be called "the dogma of religion." Guy Murchie, a scientist of no small stature, wrote a book titled *The Seven Great Mysteries of Life*. In it he wonders whether:

"Scientists were ever made aware that science can experience only what it measures, while religion may tune in on the ever-wider experience of things beyond measure."

Of course there is no proof for such a statement. Religious experiences are spiritually-bounded and can't be measured. By the same token, common sense and deductive reasoning sometimes don't make sense. We have to go deeper. We have to use what the scientists call "axiomatic" proofs. In Euclidian geometry, we learned an axiom. Remember it? "A straight line is the shortest distance between two points." This was self-evident. It needed no logic. It proved itself and, indeed, as students, we felt it to be so in our bones.

We know, as well, though, that through the science of astronomy we have learned that it is *also* true that the shortest distance between two points in *not* a straight line, but a curve. Therefore, as a matter of fact, we also learned that in order for something to *be* an axiom, it had to be unprovable. If it can be proved, it isn't an axiom, it's a theorem.

An axiom may convey a feeling of absolute conviction that it is right or true though unprovable. An intuition or knowledge deeper than thought accompanies it and this comes from the heart… not the mind.

So hold fast to those axioms, my friends. To do so it to realize that there is a profound, yet irrational quality in something that is beautiful. It needs little argument. Indeed, it should stand by itself.

I think it was the Romantic poet, John Keats who wrote in the poem "Ode to a Grecian Urn" that

"Beauty is truth, truth beauty,
that is all ye know on earth
and all ye need to know."

"*Utrum sit Deus?*" (Is there a God?) If we sometimes catch a glimpse of what sparkles in life; of what is joyous; of what is good and right in ways of serving the needs of others, it will be by seeking some concept of that presence within our lives we can gather and praise together.

A three-year-old looked wonderingly over the side of the crib at his new baby sister. Quickly, he whispered, so that no one would hear, "How was it there? Tell me. I forgot." And a parent was listening and wondered at the wisdom of the question.

Doctor Lizbeth Kubler-Ross spent much of her career studying death and dying. When she became diagnosed with cancer and was, indeed, dying, she actually became impatient for death to claim her. She said in one interview that her hearers need not to be afraid of death. It will be like the chrysalis opening out of its enclosure to spread its wings to a new existence and we needn't trouble ourselves anymore than we were able to before realizing we had been born.

Utrum sit Deus? Is there a God? *Videtur quod non.* It seems not.

The answer for each of us is, and shall remain, an open one. And that is as it should be. That is as it has been… and shall remain.

Be of Good Cheer and depart this blessed place with peaceful, loving hearts.

Amen.

TO BE OVERDONE IS
TO BE UNDONE

"Be not righteous overmuch. Why should you destroy yourself?"

- Solomon

Some years ago a situation occurred in a small Midwestern town outside Chicago. The local anti-pollution committee measured the decibels registered by the fire station siren which sounded three times daily at six a.m., noon, and six p.m. The committee discovered that the noise was higher than federal standards would allow. They insisted that the siren be silenced. It was creating "noise pollution."

The results throughout the town were entirely predictable. Kids got to school late; parents missed making lunch on time; passengers arriving home on the commuter train had to wait for spouses to meet them. And it wasn't long before the populace put up such a hue and cry that the siren was reinstated as the unseen "alarm clock" in each resident's life.

Richard Baxter, the great 17th century nonconformist was a fully practicing Puritan. In one of his essays, however, he made a very interesting remark. He stated in so many words that if the Devil could not pervert the saints through worldliness, he sought to make them "more Christian than Christ." The Evil One's overall plan was to get the saints to overdo their efforts at being good. In so doing, according to Baxter, the Devil is able to attain his goal by what is perceived as a good method rather than a bad one.

Another Puritan writer contemporary with Baxter was Walter Marshall. He observed that the precept used as our text and attributed to King Solomon is a useful principle. *Be not righteous overmuch. Why should you destroy yourself?* Marshall pointed out, for instance, that Jesus asked his disciples not to follow him into the Judgment Hall. Peter ignored this request and did so. As a result, and to save his neck, Peter found himself denying that he knew Jesus on three different occasions.

Observations such as these reveal profound insights into life. It is a bit surprising to find them coming from the pens of two distinguished Nonconformists. We usually have a different perception regarding the early Puritans. The Puritan was a religious fanatic, overdone to the point of undoing. The play titled *The Crucible* by Arthur Miller is set in the time of the Salem witch trials. It contains a host of such figures. They are not seduced by the allurements of wickedness. After all, Puritans were supposed to be immune to such possibilities. They were induced, instead, to embrace a kind of fanatical righteousness. Such were the witch trials. One need look no further in history than the Roman Catholic and Protestant Inquisitions to see the same thing.

Picture it, then. Here's this lofty-minded, black-garbed idealist Puritan symbolically bolting the front door against the evil temptations of the world. But the Devil creeps in by the back door, almost as if he were in the disguise of God. He encourages the Puritan to carry his fight to still greater heights of intensity and ferocity. He "undoes him," or rather, gets the Puritan to "undo himself" by an exhibition of overwhelming zeal, almost out of control.

Not all Puritans fit this picture. There were some who were quite aware of the dangers of an "overdone" religion. They were well versed in the knowledge of what the Scriptures contained and they understood the symbolic nature of Jesus' life. Like Baxter and Marshall, they held that Jesus was a human being, not a God. And they cautioned against going too far in seeing Jesus as perfect.

Jesus spent much of his time in the company of society's undesirable elements. His opponents were the Scribes and Pharisees, the advocates of intense righteousness. For Jesus, such a way of behavior held less hope for the world than the potential good in the lives of the sinners they publicly condemned.

Read the gospel account. In a final gesture as if to symbolize the revolutionary nature of the story, Jesus is crucified between two thieves. It was the Scribes and Pharisees who put an end to Jesus' ministry. "Underworld" characters had no hand in it at all. So you see, Puritanism is usually remembered as containing these same elements of fanaticism.

I suggest that we can cite examples today of groups and individuals who would like to see "neo-Puritanism" become a fact. They often bear the stamp of the fanatic and the overdone. In doing so, they become unwitting agents of evil.

Some are only vaguely organized. They usually serve but a single cause. Consider the tactics of what might be called the "Anti-choice" people. If you don't agree with them that abortion is evil, then you are "anti-life." So in their enthusiasm to make their point, they bomb Planned Parenthood centers and murder innocent doctors and volunteers.

Some of the most outspoken conservation groups, anti-tax groups, protectionist groups are apt to reflect the same philosophy. Usually society is not apt to take them completely seriously. But as they strive to achieve their goals, their zeal creates all kinds of spinoff problems. They condemn all who would disagree with them. Their way is the *only* way!

Think about it. What imaginary devil would not give his very eyes to have enemies such as some of the radio pundits of our day? What evil presence would have loved the likes of such extremists as David Duke or Madelyn Murray O'Hare? No matter what category, on the liberal or the conservative side, both are real gifts because they perform their overly-righteous scenarios at no cost.

How many people, upon being told by any one of a number of fanatical extremists that they should *not* see a certain movie, or read a certain book – will most certainly go right out – and as soon as possible – see that movie or read that book? And yet, the very existence of that movie or that book may never have occurred to them.

In the Middle Ages, the Church, in its zeal to encourage the faithful, resorted to many pious frauds. Count the bones of the saints in the cathedrals of Europe or the number of what are claimed as "the original Holy Grail," the cup from which Jesus drank. In those days, simple people thought they were witnessing or hearing about "miracles." Faith in God and the power of the Church was increased.

Listen to the way this scenario might have happened. The speaker is the archbishop. The play is *Saint Joan* by George Bernard Shaw.

"Parables are not lies because they describe events that never happened. Miracles are not frauds. Why? Because they often – I do not say always – are very innocent contrivances by which the priest fortifies the faith of his flock. ...If they feel the thrill of the supernatural and forget their sinful clay in a sudden sense of the glory of God – it will be a miracle, and a blessed one."

Such practices by the Church gave it prestige for a time. In the long run, such events earned it the reputation for corruption and deceit. It brought the entire institution into such disrepute that when the Church *did* try to speak truth as a religious witness in society, its voice was no longer heard.

This same kind of fraudulent practice has been taken over occasionally by some of the more well-known charities. An article in the *New Humanist* magazine once told of touched-up stories and faked pictures of misery appearing in the press advertisements they issued.

You and I know there are very real human needs in our society today. We also know that much good work is accomplished by such charities. But it would seem that some charities are not willing to rest content with presenting the true picture. They are not satisfied depicting misery as it is. No. They seem to feel that in order to extract as much money as possible; they have to paint a darker picture than is really there. They believe they have to concoct what we might call "more perfect... misery." There's an oxymoron. But true. And like the Church, the day eventually comes when such a deception is revealed and such charities also earn the reputation for dishonesty. Overdoing finally... undoes.

A famous satire was written some years ago concerning the activities of Senator Joseph McCarthy. It was called *The Investigator* and was written by Ruben Ship. Most of us can recall McCarthy's investigations in the 1950s for what was called The House Un-American Activities Committee. Under McCarthy's leadership it became all-but obsessed with the Un-American activities of many American citizens. His list contained governmental officials and private citizens, elected representatives, writers, actors, directors and others.

In the satire, McCarthy is depicted as having been involved in a plane crash on his way to an investigation. There are no survivors. He wakes to find himself being presented as an applicant to the celestial "immigration authorities." He is told that before he is allowed in that he will be investigated to see whether or not he is a desirable immigrant.

McCarthy becomes indignant. He fusses, fumes and questions the competence of the committee. Eventually he gains an audience. He forces the chairman to resign. He then takes the chairman's place and in his acceptance speech he claims that *many* undesirable elements have been admitted to heaven. This is due in no small measure to the incompetence of the former chairperson. Obviously, they must be *re*-investigated under *his* chairmanship. If necessary, some will have to be deported.

So thousands of the distinguished company of heaven are trooped before this newly-constituted committee. Many of them are found guilty of treason and immediately deported down to hell. Who are these figures? Oh, no one important. Just people like Mark Twain, Socrates, Thomas Jefferson. There are Susan B. Anthony, Martin Luther, Karl Marx, John Milton. Out go Dorothea Dix and Abraham Lincoln, too. A whole host of "unimportant people."

No one is immune – no one is too high. This disagreeable task has to be done, according to the Investigator, in the name of… "righteousness!"

What happens is that he goes too far. All those reformers and revolutionaries begin to cause disorder in hell. They proceed to set up an organization demanding rights for the damned. Their slogan becomes, "Workers of the underworld unite! You have nowhere to go… but UP!"

Suddenly there is not only the danger of a revolution in hell, but there is the added problem that heaven might be taken by storm. And, led by such a gifted group of people, it might very well succeed. So McCarthy begins to worry. He decides that it is time to call in "The Chief" himself for investigation. No one is too high – so why not… God? If God is found guilty, the Investigator can take *his* place. *He* will become the Lord of Hosts and prevent the takeover. What happens? He undoes himself.

The limits of God's patience and tolerance are finally reached. God orders McCarthy's deportation down to hell. But this can't happen. The Devil claims he has rights, too. He has no place in hell for an individual who has bungled things so badly. So the celestial immigration authorities find that, according to "the rules," if there is no place for him, and nobody wants him, McCarthy has to be returned to the place he was found dead. So he is sent back to the site of the plane wreck.

The people on earth are puzzled, indeed, to discover this person who should have been dead. They wonder at the physical impossibility of surviving such a crash. Yet, there it was. So they assume, at the end of the play, that it must have been – you guessed it – a "divine miracle!"

So there he remains – McCarthy the Investigator – returned to his original state. His vaulting ambition had caused him to overdo things to such an extent neither God nor the Devil have any use for him. He is left stranded, useless and insane.

Look at the world today. Even in less-dramatic circumstances, the law of diminishing returns becomes the consequence of overdoing things. Food is spoiled or made all but inedible by overcooking it. People have been known to fail and in so doing kill themselves after trying "too hard." If one applies too much fertilizer the garden will burn out, produce nothing. Too sever a discipline in one generation may produce too great a leniency in another.

As Ralph Waldo Emerson wrote in his essay, *Compensation* –

"Every excess causes a defect; every defect an excuse. If the government is cruel, the governor's life is not safe. If you tax too high, the revenue will yield nothing. If you make the criminal code sanguinary, juries will not convict."

Sadly, much of this is true today. Look, if you will, at the excess of zeal evident with Fox News and occasionally CNN and the generally salacious stories evident with television reporting – and – the same inability of said media to ask the correct questions regarding the health and future of our nation. We love to "overdo" on the junk and avoid the hard stuff. The wheels seem to be coming off the world! Once the top news story was whether Katie Couric would be going to CBS. Frankly… who… really… cares?!

It would seem, then, that our country is at the point of things getting completely out of hand. The constant scenario of charges and counter charges have not served our nation well and, according to many polls, it would seem that the average United States citizen is quite fed up.

Our leaders need to be concentrating on issues and events of world proportion – not upon the simple expedient of getting elected – one more time. Overdoing with their own campaigns and self-aggrandizement – and underperforming when it comes to the need of their constituencies and the American people seems to bring about our *own* undoing and the unraveling of the American Constitution.

Some might say that all this may be true but am I not preaching to the choir? We Unitarian Universalists like to think of ourselves as the very last people to be overdone. We picture ourselves as models of moderation, tolerance, balance. We try hard to hold even judgment regarding the affairs of humanity. We try to apply standards of equality and justice to one and all.

We can think of plenty of cults and sects that fit Richard Baxter's slogan of "more Christian than Christ." BUT NOT US!

Think for a moment, though. Perhaps we should not be feeling so assured regarding our brand of liberal righteousness, either. It may very well be that some of the things to which we are devoted can become overdone and distorted.

For instance, the word "freedom" is an inspiring concept. But to enjoy its blessings, a certain amount of responsibility and commitment have to be there for it to work. In order to maintain that freedom, individuals must be vigilant and really care. And this is apt to mean some inconvenience on the part of the individuals making up that organization. An overdone claim to freedom can sometimes take the shape of people owning *no* responsibility; showing *no* commitment. They are apt, under the guise of freedom, to say they can do anything, believe anything, listen only to the moment.

The enemies of freedom are not slow to take advantage of such a human tendency. This is the way the devotees of freedom are apt to play into the hands of those who would severely *limit* freedom.

It is also possible to take the principle of tolerance to extremes. As Unitarian Universalists, we have always affirmed religious tolerance. As we possess it, we would also protect it for others.

There are those religious zealots, however, for whom *their way* of thinking is the only way. Many, under the guise of tolerance, miss the more subtle points some religious leaders advocate. So if our tolerance is so overdone as to be uncritical, the results can become harmful to all.

We need, then, to use our common sense at such times. While the virtue of tolerance should be kept, we need to monitor just how far an easy tolerance might be allowed not only in the secular realm of politics, but in the sacred realm of religion.

Finally, (believe it or not) there can be an overdone devotion to moderation. In such cases one is inhibited from doing anything constructive at all. And it sometimes alarms me to hear responses from Unitarian Universalists when faced with some controversial issue; "We don't know enough about that matter to act in one way or another about it."

The founder of the philosophical school called "Skepticism" was a man named Pyrrho. He affirmed this. He said that one can never know enough to be sure that one course of action is to be preferred over another. Pyrrho's philosophy was today's "situational ethics" on steroids.

In his youth, he gained these insights from his teacher. And one day he was out walking a country road. Suddenly he came upon an old man with his head stuck in a ditch. Upon closer investigation he discovered that it was none other than his old teacher who was stuck. Pyrrho considered the situation. His teacher had taught him to review things when such eventualities occurred. So he did. He observed; he thought about it; perhaps he may even have "agonized" over it. Then, deciding that he did not know enough about it, he walked away, doing nothing.

Of course the very next group of people coming down the road was quick to pull the old man out of the ditch. But what happened the next day in the town square where the ancient Greeks would congregate? Why Pyrrho's teacher *congratulated* his pupil for being consistent with what he had been taught!

An extreme case? Of course. But it serves to remind us that we, in our devotion to freedom, tolerance and moderation must always be on guard. If our devotion is not tempered with realism and understanding, it can unwittingly be seduced just as easily as it is for the same thing to happen to the self-righteous neo-Puritan or fanatical fundamentalist.

We would like to say, I am sure, that our lives are dedicated to preserving and enhancing the ideals bought for us in blood by our spiritual mothers and fathers of an earlier religious age. Occasionally, however, we need to remind ourselves of some important guidelines in serving our faith… our Unitarian Universalism.

When our freedom becomes license; when our tolerance becomes blind to reality; when our moderation becomes apathy – then our light of faith is dimmed. And if that light goes out in this old world, that light of freedom, reason and truth, then how great could be the darkness that follows.

The choice is always ours. (Wrote Aldous Huxley.) *Then let me choose*
The longest art, the hard Promethean way
Cherishingly to tend and feed and fan
That inward fire, whose small precarious flame,
Kindled or quenched, creates
The noble or ignoble persons we are,
The worlds we live in and the very fates,
Our bright or muddy star.

THE IDEA OF HELL

Comment: Robert Ingersoll was a lawyer, orator and preacher during the years of the American Freethought Movement. Here is an excerpt from his lecture which he titled "Heretics and Heresies."

It is claimed that God wrote a book called the Bible, and it is generally admitted that this book is somewhat difficult to understand. As long as the Church had all the copies of this book, and the people were not allowed to read it, there was comparatively little heresy in the world; but when it was printed and read; people began honestly to differ as to its meaning.

A few were independent and brave enough to give the world their real thoughts, and for the extermination of these (free thinkers), the Church used all her power. Protestants and Catholics vied with each other in the work of enslaving the human mind. For ages they were rivals in the infamous effort to rid the earth of honest people. They appealed to the worst passions of the human heart. They sowed the seeds of discord and hatred in every land. Brother denounced brother, wives informed against their husbands, mothers accused their children, dungeons were crowded with the innocent; the flesh of the good and true rotted in the clasp of chains; the flames devoured the heroic, and in the name of the most merciful God, his children were exterminated with famine, sword and fire.

Over the wild waves of battle rose and fell the banner of Jesus Christ. For sixteen hundred years the robes of the Church were red with innocent blood. The ingenuity of Christians was exhausted in devising punishment severe enough to be inflicted upon other Christians who honestly and sincerely differed with them upon any point whatever.

Give any orthodox church the power, and today they would punish heresy with whip, and chain and fire. As long as a church deems a certain belief essential to salvation, just so long it will kill and burn if it has the power.

So, in conclusion we say, "Thank you, Robert Ingersoll!"

BASEBALL AS GOSPEL TRUTH

"The test of a good religion – whether you can joke about it."
- G. K. Chesterton

The headline of the *Boston Globe* on October 10, 2000 said it all. **For Sale: Olde Town Team**. The story told of the announcement made by CEO John Harrington to put the Boston Red Sox on the market for sale. For many, the news portended a season of change and uncertainty until a new owner or owners could be named. So fans today, having assumed the Red Sox would be New England based for all time, are now saying, "Where will it all end?" But those of us who consider ourselves members of the Red Sox Nation know the answer to that as we sit here today, don't we? The Red Sox are again trying for the Championship.

David R. Carlin writes a column for *Commonweal* magazine. In one he wrote about running for the Rhode Island Senate. He did this every two years. The job is thankless; paying $300 per year for a session that lasts from January to June. Carlin claimed remarkable success with his campaign because he tied his political concerns to the Rhode Island voter's preoccupation with the triumphs and pitfalls of the Boston Red Sox. Only incidentally did they seem preoccupied with the arms race, the national debt or the war in Iraq or the continuing Mid-East crises.

"Such is the nature of American politics as House Speaker Tip O'Neill advised, and went on to say that *all* politics is local politics. Baseball, then, for many, is a way of life that has the stuff of religion about it."

It was in reading that article that I decided to attempt a sermon on baseball. After all, many of my colleagues do it. In fact, one whole issue of a denominational quarterly was dedicated to the topic.

Tradition has it that in 1839, one Abner Doubleday laid out the first baseball diamond in Elihu Phinney's pasture in Cooperstown, New York.

There, with a cloth-stuffed, stitched leather sphere, he conducted the first baseball game ever played. The players were cadets of the military preparatory school where Doubleday was stationed as an instructor. Obviously, opinions about the beginning of the sport vary. But if you were to play a word association game, I assure you that if someone were to say the word Cooperstown, the immediate response would be "Baseball" – which indicates something of the ubiquitous nature of our national pastime.

Each year an annual rite involves this odyssey of sport. Seldom equaled in any other sporting event, it called The World Series of Baseball for the Championship of the World. It is time, then, given the impending struggle again between the Boston Red Sox and the New York Yankees, to speak of baseball.

One of my favorite movies is titled *Bull Durham*. A major premise of that film – a film actually of a charming love story – is that some people will live under any conditions in order to play professional baseball. But the same holds true for amateurs. It was so of myself as a boy in southern Alabama.

Susan Sarandon plays the narrative figure in the movie. She is a baseball devotee. At the beginning, as she lights the candles in her little shrine to baseball, she says, "There are 108 beads on a rosary and 108 stitches in a baseball… and the only church that really feeds the soul, day in and day out, is the Church of Baseball."

In some respects her statement is true. There are dimensions to baseball that make it a reflection of life. It is difficult to avoid making the comparison. There is a fluidity to the game – like the motion of a month gone by – or a day spent at leisure in the mountains. There is a pattern to it – batting, throwing, running the bases. They converge in the same sense as do the ancient celebrations of birth, coming-of-age, marriage and death. The dimension of time moves differently in a ballpark. Time is not marked by a clock, but by innings.

Uniquely, then, baseball presents a kind of seamless and invisible mode. A single game is a neatly-contained world which moves exactly as each of its predecessors. Metaphorically, it resembles, then, the continuance of a human life from parent to child to grandchild.

Baseball is played in much the same way today as it was in the days of our youth. Somehow those were slower times. Life was simpler – or so it seemed. And, since any game is measured in outs all one had to do to succeed was to keep hitting, keep the rally alive. Success and victory were attained. And so, in such a way one defeats time, if only for the blur of a moment.

Realizing some of you may wonder at the seemingly non-religious nature of what I am saying, I would like to defend myself. Let me take you on a journey of remembrance. Depart the "here and now" and allow yourselves some simple reveries. You may not have played the sport at all but that doesn't matter. For baseball is just a euphemism. It is a way of nourishing the human soul. We call it "play."

In an exceptional essay titled "Why Time Begins On Opening Day," a modern author with the well-known name of Thomas Boswell wrote:

"Baseball isn't necessarily an escape from reality, though it can be; it's merely one of our many refuges within the real where we try to create a sense of order on our own terms…"

In other words, when we engage in any kind of play, competitive or non-competitive, we set up a kind of separate cosmos. Two things occur. We observe definite rules and we suspend time. We do this by leaving the commonplace; that world of fear, pain, the serious world. Time becomes an interval or an inning… or an out. Space… is the playing area. But space is circumscribed. All around it are those who support the concept called "play" and they are the spectators. And… unlike the tedious nature of the everyday, play ends. But one is never sure when or at what time or under what circumstances. For after all, it was the immortal Yogi Berra, a virtual legend in his own time, who said that "It ain't over 'til it's over!"

Yogi Berra (aka Lawrence Peter Berra) was a baseball player whose major career position was played as a catcher for the New York Yankees. He was born in Saint Louis on the same street as professional catcher, and later baseball announcer, Joe Garagiola. They grew up together. Following his Yankee years, Yogi later became a coach and then team manager. But Yogi was more than this. Not only was he a singularly gifted athlete, he was a man whose career spanned a kind of golden age of excellence in the sport.

Obviously in those days there were problems with the league and with the players – alcohol abuse, greed, gambling, irresponsibility. But when you consider such singular gatherings as the Saint Louis Cardinals bunch they called "The Gas House Gang" – then a whimsical chord rings in the memory of all who read or witnessed the antics of those "boys of summer."

There was little or nothing of player strikes in those days. There were no franchise maneuverings, no steroid doping, no drug scandal or spousal abuse cases. Obviously there was occasional violence on the field and betting on games and in the stands went on all the time. But spitting at umpires and some of the other sad qualities that denote the modern player and team were not there.

Oh, yes, I know about the famous Black Sox Scandal of 1919 with the Chicago White Sox. But notwithstanding that brief encounter there seemed a kind of purity in the sport. I remember players such as Casey Stengel, Joe DiMaggio, Ted Williams, Stan Musial and Whitey Ford. And I recall especially the Jackie Robinsons, the Don Newcombes and the Willie Mays of baseball.

While serving as Interim Minister of the Santa Fe congregation I came to know ninety-one year old John Pierce. John played professional baseball before the Depression for the first Negro Professional Baseball League. He had been a member of the Unitarian Church of Santa Fe for many years.

John was on the Indianapolis ABCs Ballclub and paid his way through college playing as a second baseman. There was a lot of barnstorming in those days, not to mention wild exhibition games played between white major league teams and black professional teams. In John's day, the Yankees of the Negro League were the Kansas City Monarchs. He said his team once played against the indomitable New York Yankees (Jimmy Fox, Lou Gehrig, Babe Ruth)… and the Monarchs *beat* the Yankees… handily. According to John, the then Commissioner of Baseball, a white man of course, made a rule that hence forth there would be no exhibition games between white and Negro baseball teams. John said that in those days gambling went on all the time – but not with the players – in the stands. And if someone made an excellent play, spectators would throw money out onto the field for the hero making the play.

Simply put, then, baseball was a game. It was human play that everyone could do to a greater or lesser extent. All one needed was a bat and a ball… and kids often made their own balls out of any number of ingredients.

Later in his young life during World War II, John Pierce became a member of what became known as the "Tuskegee Airmen," the 99th Fighter Squadron of the United States Army Air Force.

Back to Yogi Berra. Berra, as some of you might have suspected, was a kind of left-handed philosopher. He was once described as a guy who "walked like a yogi." But it wasn't his athletic skills so much as it was *his linguistic canards* that made him, like the immortal Dizzy Dean before him, an exemplary spokesman for the game. Here are a few examples.

In speaking about his new house: "It's nothing but rooms." Giving directions *to* his new home: "It's pretty far, but it doesn't seem like it." On being told by New York Mayor John Lindsey's wife that he looked very cool in his summer suit: "Thanks. You don't look so hot yourself." How about this one? On seeing the movie *Doctor Zhivago* he remarked that "It sure was cold in Russia in those days."

People used to poke fun at Yogi for his habit of reading comic books. He once responded with: "If it's so silly, how come every time I put one down, somebody else picks it up?!" One of my favorites is: "If the people don't want to come out to the ballpark, nobody's going to stop them!" His acceptance speech on Yogi Berra Day started with these words: "I want to thank everybody who made this day necessary."

Yogi did have a way with words, didn't he? One season he had a roommate who was a medical student. When they were in their hotel room the young man would always be studying. On one occasion as he finished reading a textbook on human anatomy, Yogi looked over at him and said, "How did it come out?"

What does one say about such verbal versatility? Truly, Yogi was a man for all seasons. And how can *I not* say such a thing? For was it not Yogi who said things like "You can observe a lot… by watching!" Then, this man, using elementary logic said, "How can that pitcher stay in the majors considering the stuff he keeps striking me out with?!"

In many ways, then, baseball was a major portion of my young life. Though I never saw a major league game or stepped into a major league park until well into my teens, for me, the major leagues were a dream world. They existed over the scratchy speaker of our home radio or my crystal radio set I'd listen to under the covers with my brother after we were supposed to have gone to bed.

Baseball was something you played. It was carefully hammering tiny wire brads into a split bat, then, even more carefully, wrapping black electrician's tape – the old kind, not the smooth plastic stuff – around the handle. Baseball was dusty fields and rocks for bases. It was "Choose 'em Up" with one getting the eagle's clutch at the top of the bat winning first choice of players.

My friends were Billy and Bobby, Robert and Sonny and my brother Peter. We also played with boys whose nicknames strained human credibility; "Pork," who obviously played catcher; "Lard," "Simp," "Rascal," "Toothpick," "Fish" and "Tatorhead." Baseball for us was the act of playing whenever we got the chance. For someone to show up with a new ball was heaven. The height of boredom was to stand in the outfield while the pitcher failed, time after time, to get the ball near the batter.

Most of all, however, it was John D. Miller Memorial Ball Park, home of the Brewton Millers (named after the lumber mill John Miller had owned and which supported the town team.) The Millers in those days were a class D professional ball team of the Southern Alabama League.

On at least sixty nights during the summer, we kids would work for the concession manager. On summer evenings when the team was in town we would hawk peanuts, popcorn, soda pop and candy to the crowd. And the town came out in droves. After all, next to the Ritz movie *thee-a-ter*, baseball was the only other event in that town of 2500 inhabitants.

The proudest summer of my boyhood was when I was chosen bat boy for the team. I am sure that Larry Cianciola had something to do with that. Larry Cianciola was the left fielder for the team. He had shown up one Sunday at the Universalist Church where my Dad was Minister. The liberal faith appealed to Larry, a lapsed-Catholic from Cleveland. When it came time for he and his fiancé Laverne to get married, he asked Dad to perform the ceremony.

In the Brewton ballpark an actual scene reminiscent of one in the movie *Bull Durham* took place. Larry and Laverne were married at home plate before the beginning of the first playoff game at season's end. Now I've done some pretty unusual wedding scenarios but I suspect I will never equal the singular quality of that evening. There I was in my bat boy's uniform. Nervously, I watched as my father walked to home plate in his pulpit robe. I heard him over the public address system as he pronounced the solemn vows of matrimony for that young couple.

I will also never forget the conclusion of that event. In a kind of slow-motion happening, three things seemed to occur simultaneously. Dad pronounced them husband and wife and started for the stands; Larry kissed Laverne, pulled his glove out of his back uniform pocket, gave it a whack and started for his position in the outfield and the umpire turned toward the stand and, almost impatiently, shouted, "Play ball!"

That was Baseball as Gospel Truth! – something so rich in human meaning; so filled with honest emotions; so true of the best in rural American life that I will always be able to recall it and celebrate it.

Today, notwithstanding the modernization of the game, it somehow remains the same for me. Baseball is a kind of inner game or play one can return to at any time. It has no season. One can play the game of comparisons in an endless procession of baseball greats – Babe Ruth – how would he have batted against Nolan Ryan? Carl Hubbell – could he have bested the bat of Ted Williams? In the mind's eye it is remembering the graceful lope of Joe DiMaggio hauling in a long fly ball or "Say Hey" Willie Mays catching a ball over his shoulder with his familiar basket catch, falling, rolling and then getting up and throwing the ball to the infield.

When one recalls such feats it is clear the sport can never be boring or slow notwithstanding current efforts to hurry it up. The game is watched – watched intensely by those who understand it. It forces a kind of focus on even the most uninitiated. And, too, we know there is another side to it all. Someone... one side or the other, is going to fail. Someone is going to have to shoulder the blame; a pitcher hangs a sliding curve ball that is hammered into a home run; a catcher lets the pitch get by and a run scores; a fielder boots an easy grounder or fly permitting a base runner. Someone... will surely end up the loser even if it's the whole team that fails to get a hit.

In a baseball game, tension can become so real that as failure is avoided again and again we sit in relief. Then, something happens. We rise and cry out. Inevitable, irresistible, spontaneous, almost a universal cry for life.

So you see, my friends, baseball can be seen as the purity of the gifted athlete; crouched, ready to go back on a hard grounder or charging in on a surprise bunt; it is watching the arc of a base hit *and* watching the coach at the same time gauging the speed of the runner and the throw from the outfielder. Baseball is total joy in seeing a home run lifted so high and far angels seem to sing. It is the dark, black depression of that last inning double play to end a rally and plunge your team to defeat.

In Peter Berber's fine book, *A Rumor of Angels*, he suggests theologians and religious writers ought to seek out what he calls "signals of transcendence" within human experience. He suggests that the reader try to find things and experiences in the natural world that actually point beyond themselves. In reflecting on these everyday events, we come to the conclusion that, by their very nature, they raise themselves above the ordinary but need not be compared with anything "supernatural."

I believe baseball has that enigma about it. It confronts us with the reality of natural law and inevitable consequences. When a pitcher cheats on the hitter by trying to use a spitball, and he's caught, the law of the game intervenes. When tension is released in the completion of a play, it takes on a transcendence that is timeless. Baseball, like a mirror, reflects not only dreams come true, but the law of consequences. You can play the "what if" game all you want but the figures in the record book still stand.

Once, I dreamed that the day would come when I would be able to play in the major leagues. I had two heroes – the player/manager of the Cleveland Indians, Lou Boudreau, a shortstop, and Ted Williams, "the Kid," the "Splendid Splinter," and for some the greatest hitter who ever lived. I wanted to hit like Williams, field like Boudreau and to play in Fenway Park. My grandmother Quigley was a Red Sox fan who knew all the current Red Sox statistics. She once sent me a picture of Fenway and that picture caused me, in my fantasy, to adopt that team.

As time went on it became progressively clear I would never play in the majors. But I had this internal narrative that would occur from time to time. So now, in deference to baseball in particular and to sport in general, and to the dream every child has of excelling in some manner of play in their lives; I want to dedicate this closing journey of the mind, this personal stream of consciousness, to them.

It is, very simply, a story of my life and work. Imagine, if you will, a train station. A locomotive comes steaming and chug-chugging into view.

Then a public address announcer says, "Your attention, please. Train from Pasadena, California leaving for all points east and west."

Year 1934. Baby Jan on board with parents, Richard and Rosalie. Country in depression but show biz parents ready and waiting (choo – choo). First stop, Hollywood, then Berkeley and San Jose. Asthma attacks and a look at early death. Country at war; blackouts and victory gardens. Baseball in mothballs.

"Attention, next stop, Brew-ton, Alabama."

First bat and glove – the major leagues are back in style. Listen on the radio and imagine the game. Time for dreamers and all who play the game: "Golly, Ty Cobb, Babe Ruth, Joe DiMaggio. Maybe someday I'll play shortstop in Fenway Park..."

Next stop, college. Time for dreaming to cease. This stop in the fifties. Korean War is on. Ted Williams takes time in jets to defend his country. Now baseball is an everyday reality. Read the papers. See it on television. Bobby Thompson's homer wins the pennant for the Giants. Still play the game – keep the old glove, dream the old dream...

Time for Graduate School at Oxford. In Europe; Suez Canal crisis and the beginning of the Cold War. Back home Senator McCarthy hearings; *Brown vs. Board of Education*. This stop for students, thinkers, young lovers beginning life. This wonderful world of Eisenhower. Graduate... get a job... get ahead... buy insurance... save money... own a car...

Next stop, New England. Providence only forty-five miles from Fenway. I'm really there! This station for starting a career, falling in love, marrying and beginning a family. Once in a while a trip to actually *see* the Red Sox play...

All aboard for "Mass-achusetts," next stop in the calendar of churches. Trips to black empowerment, Martin Luther King's leadership and trip to Selma, Alabama. This is the station where our first two kids, Keith and Kristan begin their lives...

Next station, Dedham, Massachusetts, home of the beginnings of Unitarianism in America; the 1967 pennant, Carl Yastrzemski and the World Series that ended 4 -3 the wrong way... Stops here at the Peace Movement, LRY, flower children, refugees from Haight Ashbury, runaways, black brothers and sisters, peace marches against the war, prayer vigils and illegal abortion counseling and *Roe vs. Wade.* Two more passengers join the Knost family train – Jana and Amy Kate...

Next stop, Summit, New Jersey, Yankee and Shea Stadiums, home of the real Brooklyn Dodgers now gone to California. College begins for kids, worry continues for parents. Growth and change come hard – we've reached the age of fifty and even softball is hard to play...

Next stops, San Antonio and Houston, Texas. Baseball and dreams so far from home...

This is a station for later age, for slowing down, thinking about the past, writing poetry and prose, trying to tell life's story.

Whoa! A siding in hospitals. Near death again with four surgeries. Recovery and try at retirement. Another chance to work in ministry and interim ministries. A new way of serving people and the gratitude of feeling validation...

Then stop, Santa Fe, New Mexico... a place of enchantment and wonder... of mountains and ancient lore... of warm people and a new time of challenge...

Next stop, our spiritual home – New England and Rhode Island – South County and Charlestown – a home for centuries to Unitarians and Universalists from near and far. Arrive as strangers to know the genuine warmth of Yankee charm and humor – a blessed place for work and worship with new friends.

Then... finally... someday... the announcer will say. "Last stop... end of the line... end of life... all out for all passengers, though Bodhisattvas can remain on board."

(Baseball still a dream...)

Question: What's a Bodhisattva?

Answer: A descendent from heaven come to earth to assist others...

Question: Can I be a bodhisattva?

Answer: Yes. Anyone can if they so choose.

Question: You mean I can come back to live again?

Answer: Yes, according to Hindu and Buddhist teaching...

Maybe... maybe... FENWAY!... FRIENDLY FENWAY!... Wow! Yes! *I still* might be a ballplayer in Fenway Park! "Play ball!"

Amen.

ACKNOWLEDGEMENTS

The author is indebted to the following friends and family for assisting him in bringing this volume to you.

To **James Conroy**, my editor, for his expertise, his constancy and his brilliance in helping me to avoid publication pitfalls.

To our daughter, **Jana Knost Battiloro**, whose Foreword is brilliant and difficult for her old man to read each time without tears.

To **Cliff Vanover**, a published author in his own right, for his early and often encouragement to assist me in the process. May his tribe increase!

To my son-in-law, **Patrick Connor Jr.**, for his talents given me in setting up my computer so I could proceed apace with the project.

To my **colleagues and friends** who've given me a lifetime of adventure, experience and wisdom which is a large part of this book.

And lastly, to my bride, my wife, my spouse, my partner and friend of over 53 years, my **Lorna**, for her counsel and quiet standing by while I ran around in every direction at once trying to make a book for my grandchildren come true.

Love you all.

Reverend Jan Vickery Knost
Charlestown, RI
August 6, 2015

CPSIA information can be obtained
at www.ICGtesting.com
Printed in the USA
BVHW030217220819
556515BV00001B/39/P